INTRODUCTION TO
RESTORATION MINISTRIES

*There's a Movement throughout the World
to Restore the Foundational Principles of the Early Church.*

Why Now?

Because God Keeps His Promises!

It hasn't gone unnoticed in the last fifty years that God is fulfilling His promises to the Jewish people as He restores them to Israel. *"Therefore say: 'This is what the Sovereign LORD says: "I will gather you from the nations and bring you back from the countries where you have been scattered, and I will give you back the land of Israel again"'"*(Ezekiel 11:17).

Through His compassionate mercy, the Lord is also restoring the Hebraic foundations of the early Church. Jesus Christ (*Yeshua Ha Mashiach*) came in the fullness of time *"to give his people the knowledge of salvation through the forgiveness of their sins, because of the tender mercy of our God, by which the rising sun will come to us from heaven"*(Luke 1:77,78). Now, in conjunction with the "tender mercy of our God" to the Jewish people, the Hebraic foundations are being restored to a Gentile Church around the world.

The Purpose of Restoration Ministries

Biblical Basis #1 for the Restoration
"Repent, then, and turn to God, so that your sins may be wiped out, that times of refreshing may come from the Lord, and that he may send the Christ, who has been appointed for you—even Jesus. He must remain in heaven until the time comes for God to restore everything, as he promised long ago through his holy prophets" (Acts 3:19-21).

God's Purpose for Restoration Ministries:

1. Awareness

Proclaiming through written word and instruction the Hebraic foundations of thought and practice upon which the early Church was founded.

2. Equipping

Enabling God's people to live out the restorative truths so that His purposes may be fulfilled in and through His people.

Each of the books and training materials produced by Restoration Ministries is one segment of a *family of information* related to the Restoration. Each publication is designed to stand alone and to equip the followers of Jesus to apply these truths and principles to their lives. The real strength of each publication is found in both its content and its interrelationship to the other facets of the restoration.

The Hebraic Priorities of the Early Church

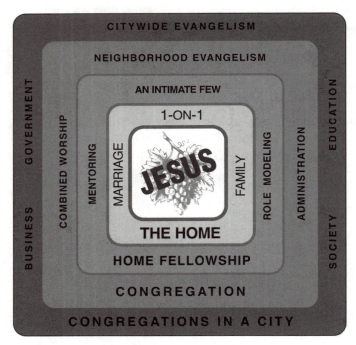

The above diagram represents the Hebraic priorities of the early Church. These priorities begin with Jesus at the center and flow out from there.

PRIORITY #1 — JESUS AND YOU

A biblically Hebraic understanding of your relationship with Jesus as a *pilgrimage* begins with the day you lovingly put your full trust and reliance in Him as Lord of your life. Unflagging trust in His Lordship and faith-filled obedience to His Word reveal His undeniable reality to you as His disciple. Only through an ongoing walk in the love of Jesus can you love others in the manner He has prescribed. The publications of Restoration Ministries are worthless to you without the centrality of a loving trust in Jesus as the focus of your life. Only the Holy Spirit can accomplish this in you and empower you to live a life of love, endurance, patience, and thanksgiving (see Col. 1:10,11).

Please stop and pray! It is extremely important that you prayerfully establish this foundation of loving trust in Jesus Christ and assurance in His Gospel before you read on.

PRIORITY #2 — YOUR HOME:

A. Marriage — The Christ Whom you seek to penetrate all your relationships needs to be present first in your home. The essence of a Hebraic-Christian marriage of the early Church could be, *"If you want to know the extent of my relationship with Jesus Christ, look for it in the love He has given me for my spouse."* God desires couples to view the love in their marriage as a visible representation of their relationship with Jesus. So vital an illustration of intimacy is marriage that God refers to Himself as the husband of His wife Israel. Jesus is called the Bridegroom of His Bride, the Church. Just as marital love is a commitment meant to deepen and grow throughout the marriage, so is union with the Holy Spirit meant to increasingly draw the believer (whether single or married) into deeper trust in God. God has designed a husband to draw strength from his wife, his nurturing companion. She is the suitable life partner given him by God to complement him as they follow God's purposes and plans together.

B. Family — God is restoring the home as the *primary building block* for Christian growth. The Jewish believers of the early Church recognized that their relationship with their Lord and the relationships in their homes were inseparably linked: *"Love the Lord your God with all your heart and with all your soul and with all your strength. These commandments that I give you today are to be upon your hearts. Impress them on your children. Talk about them when you sit at home and when you walk along the road, when you lie down and when you get up"*(Deuteronomy 6:5-7). Children are a heritage and reward from the Lord. Fathers are to *"bring them up in the training and instruction of the Lord"*(Ephesians 6:4). God's purpose for a child is best guided by parents who know their children's personalities and inclinations intimately. Such profound awareness guides parents to shepherd their children into the life decisions and vocation just right for each of them. *Shalom beit*, the peace and harmony of the home, is an essential goal for each believer. A home should be a refuge and sanctuary for each family member.

PRIORITY #3 — YOUR HOME FELLOWSHIP

God is reestablishing a key element of the early Church: the home fellowship as an *extension of the home* for spiritual growth and supportive relationships. The earliest believers met in homes with glad and sincere hearts to break bread and to *"spur one another on toward love and good deeds"*(Hebrews 10:24). The home fellowship relationship of the early Church is a seven-day-a-week commitment to one another. Key purposes of a home fellowship are to support and uphold righteousness, and to develop increasingly supportive relationships that point each other toward greater dependency on God. Marriages and families torn apart by death or divorce can be nurtured in the "extended family" of the home fellowship. Within this environment mentoring by sages and role modeling by those who have lived a life for Christ can guide those younger in their walk with the Lord. Through the family and home fellowships, God is restoring sacrificial load-bearing love to relationships. The nation of Israel's ability to respond to God's purposes was based on their relational progression from individual, to family, to clan, to the twelve tribes that comprised the nation. Following this pattern, the Church is built on the individual, family, home fellowship, congregation, and congregations throughout a city. The ultimate outpouring of this relational model into their city will enable congregations to impact their society, education system, business spheres, and government.

The Jewish People

God has promised great blessing to those who bless the seed of Abraham, the Jewish people. Over 80% of His promises to the Jews regarding their restoration to Israel have already been fulfilled. When God pours out on them a *"spirit of grace and supplication"* (Zechariah 12:10), they will be cleansed and will see Jesus the Messiah (*Yeshua Ha Mashiach*) as Lord. The Gentile Christian community must remember Paul's warning; *"I do not want you to be ignorant of this mystery, brothers, so that you may not be conceited: Israel has experienced a hardening in part until the full number of the Gentiles has come in"*(Romans 11:25). Gentile believers can pray, and through humility, work to undo the past injustices carried out by the Church against the Jewish people.

Biblical Basis #2 for the Restoration
"I will bend Judah as I bend my bow and fill it with Ephraim. I will raise up your sons, O Zion, against your sons, O Greece, and make you like a warrior's sword" (Zechariah 9:13).

Hebraic Practices of the Early Church

Throughout the world the Lord is sending forth a Hebraic spirit to undo the Greek spirit that has held the Gentile Christian Church captive for centuries. By the third century many anti-Semitic writings and practices had entered the Church through the teachings and philosophical influences of converted Greek philosophers. Attempts to reconcile Plato and Christianity replaced the Hebraic foundations that had strengthened the early Church. Philosophy and its cognitive, theoretical approach to life entered the Church and subordinated a trusting and obedient relationship with the Lord of life. Paul had warned the Church against this: *"See to it that no one takes you captive through hollow and deceptive philosophy, which depends on human tradition and the basic principles of this world rather than on Christ"*(Colossians 2:8). Many of the so-called doctrines that now divide God's children are a result of the infiltration of Greek philosophy. The early Church would have understood "doctrine" to be the message of truth for which one would be willing to die, rather than persecute and despise others for whom Jesus shed His precious blood. *"All of us who are mature should take such a view of things. And if on some point you think differently, that too God will make clear to you. Only let us live up to [the love we have already attained]"* (Philippians 3:15,16).

Living Out God's Word
A Hebraic-Greek Comparison

Hebraic
Active—appeals to the heart

Process Oriented
- Stresses direct participation
- Emphasizes age and wisdom
- Role modeling, mentoring, and discipleship indispensable
- Leadership by personal example
- Character of leader essential
- Personal relationships imperative

Biblical Application
- Doers of the Word
- Bible—reality that must be confronted
- Goal—to develop Christlikeness

Ministry Activity
- Small intimate groups
- Leader as facilitator
- Cooperative, participatory planning
- Spiritual gifts shared
- Frequent scheduled and unscheduled gatherings

Fruit
- Love, acceptance, forgiveness
- Transparency encouraged
- Active participation
- "How you serve" vital
- Each believer trained to serve
- Produces mature believers

Greek
Cognitive—appeals to the intellect

Program Oriented
- Heavy program prominence
- Emphasizes education
- Relies on speaking skills, oratory, programmed materials, information conveyance
- Leader's personal life immaterial
- Personal relationships optional

Biblical Application
- Belief without personal cost
- Bible—data that must be taught
- Focus on rules—do's and don'ts
- Emphasizes distinct denominations

Ministry Activity
- Large impersonal groups
- Leader-directed and controlled
- Organizational roles important
- Acquisition of knowledge emphasized
- Reliance on scheduled gatherings

Fruit
- Mutual toleration
- Transparency discouraged
- Passivity and lethargy
- "What you know" vital
- Trained professionals utilized
- Produces spectators

A Word of Encouragement

Jesus encouraged all who would follow Him, "I will build my church". No church can be built unless Jesus is the Cornerstone. Church life and practice must once again encompass the foundational Hebraic understanding upon which the apostles and the writers of the New Testament built. The influence of Greek theory and philosophy, and the centuries of anti-Semitism in the church have hindered our return to our Hebraic roots. The church of Jesus Christ was never meant to be divided by human commands, traditions, and knowledge. As the Restoration continues, the church will be built upon Jesus, living by the power of His Spirit, and manifesting the trusting obedience of the God-fearing Jews who committed their lives to the Messiah Jesus in the early Church.

May God bless you as you incorporate this material into your life through the power of His Spirit for the glory of Jesus Who alone is worthy of all glory.

Demolishing Strongholds

Mike and Sue Dowgiewicz

God's Way to Mental Freedom

Aslan Group
PUBLISHING

3595 Webb Bridge Rd. • Alpharetta, GA 30202 • 770-442-1500

Unless otherwise stated, Scripture taken from the
Holy Bible, New International Version©.
Copyright© 1978,1984 by International Bible Society.
Used by permission of Zondervan Publishing House. All rights reserved.

The "NIV" and "New International Version" trademarks are
registered in the United States Patent and Trademark Office by
International Bible Society. Use of either trademark requires the
permission of International Bible Society.

Scripture quotations marked KJV are from the King James Version.

Scripture quotations marked RSV are from the Revised Standard Version,
copyright© 1952, Division of Christian Education of the
National Council of Churches of Christ in the United States of America.

All rights reserved
Printed in the United States of America

ISBN 1-888582-00-6

Copyright © 1995 Mike & Sue Dowgiewicz

Aslan Group Publishing
3595 Webb Bridge Road
Alpharetta, Georgia 30202
(770) 442-1500 FAX (770) 442-1844

Contents

Introduction to Restoration Ministries .... *I*

Biography and Acknowledgement *4*

Preface *5*

Chapter One
Creation: God Created Us with Seven Needs
(Genesis 1 and 2) *9*

Chapter Two
The Demonic Forces in Strongholds *19*

Chapter Three
How Adam's Fall into Sin Has Harmed Us
(Genesis 3:1-4:7) *29*

Chapter Four
Steps To Identify and Demolish Strongholds *35*

Overview of Types of Strongholds *37*

Chapter Five
Taking Back Surrendered Ground *55*

Conclusion *65*

Restoration Ministries: Mission and Purpose *66*

About the Authors

Mike Dowgiewicz, president of *Restoration Ministries,* a ministry of *Christian Conciliation Service of Atlanta, Inc.,* and his wife Sue administrated a church retreat center where for ten years they taught over 5,000 people from a variety of churches and denominations. While at the center, Mike was a counselor to pastors and church leaders throughout southern New England. Their ministry was recognized by the Associated Press in an article that was published nationally. Mike also was featured in an article in *New England Church Life*, "Who Pastors the Pastor?"

Before his retreat center ministry, Mike was a career officer in the Navy, having served on three deployments to Vietnam as a helicopter pilot. While he was in the Navy he gave his life to Jesus. Sue made that same commitment a few months later.

Mike and Sue reside in Alpharetta, Georgia. They have one son, Sean Michael.

Restoration Ministries has its basis in research they did while living in Israel for three months during 1993-94. Through *Restoration Ministries* they are now sharing God's re-establishment of the priorities that strengthened the early Christians.

Mike holds a B.A. in Economics from the University of Connecticut, an MBA from California Lutheran College, and a Master of Religious Education from Gordon-Conwell Theological Seminary. Sue holds a B.S. in Education from the University of Connecticut.

Acknowledgement

We gratefully acknowledge the help of Mark Santostefano, who first introduced us to the biblical understanding of spiritual strongholds. We also extend warm thanks to our special friend Os Hillman and to the Aslan Group, brothers and sisters who encouraged us to keep sharing this message and helped us put it all together. And thank you, Tris Sevdy, for the long commutes to work on the revision. Above all, we thank our Lord God Who is the Author and Finisher of our faith, Who has joined us together with all other believers in His Body to work in unity for His glory.

We dedicate this book to our mothers, Mary Dowgiewicz and Rosmar Goodrich, two wonderful women who stood by us and believed in us.

PREFACE

Through our teaching retreat ministry, my wife Sue and I have helped several thousand people demolish the **spiritual strongholds*** that have hindered and hurt them for so long. We have seen the fruit of lives changed, relationships healed, and in some cases, medical symptoms eradicated when the influence of various strongholds has been eliminated.

As you go through this book, keep in mind that we are not espousing a prayer technique; we are **appropriating the authority represented in the name of the Lord Jesus Christ.** Behind His Name is the summation of all authority in the universe.

> *"Then Jesus came to them and said, 'All authority in heaven and on earth has been given to me"* (Matthew 28:18).

> *"Therefore God exalted him [Jesus] to the highest place and gave him the name that is above every name, that at the name of Jesus every knee should bow, in heaven and on earth and under the earth, and every tongue confess that Jesus Christ is Lord, to the glory of God the Father"* (Philippians 2:9-11).

> *"And having disarmed the powers and authorities, [Jesus] made a public spectacle of them, triumphing over them by the cross"* (Colossians 2:15).

*Strongholds: internal fortresses of influence from which demonic spirits agitate, oppress and afflict individuals. These spirits arouse and incline attitudes and actions that are contrary to the will of God.
(See Chapter 2 for further explanation.)

The spiritual forces of evil — demons — are fallen angels whom God cast down to the earth from heaven (see Revelation 12:9). **They are subject to Jesus Christ, Who has given us authority in His name to demolish their influence in our lives.** As evangelist Ed Silvoso says, "Serve them eviction notices."

References pertaining to **specific types of spirits** — or to the capability of demonic spirits to influence individuals in specific ways — abound in Scripture.

Examine this sampling of verses.

> *"The Spirit clearly says that in later times some will abandon the faith and follow **deceiving spirits** and things taught by demons"* (1Timothy 4:1, emphasis added).

> *"To appoint unto them that mourn in Zion...the garment of praise for the **spirit of heaviness**"* (Isaiah 61:3, KJV, emphasis added).

> *"For ye have not received the **spirit of bondage** again **to fear**, but ye have received the Spirit of adoption, whereby we cry, 'Abba, Father'"* (Romans 8:15, KJV, emphasis added).

> *"As for you, you were dead in your transgressions and sins, in which you used to live when you followed the ways of this world and of the ruler of the kingdom of the air, the **spirit who is now at work in those who are disobedient**"* (Ephesians 2:1,2, emphasis added).

> *"And the **spirit of jealousy** come upon him, and he be jealous of his wife, and she be defiled"* (Numbers 5:14, KJV, emphasis added).

> *"Dear children, this is the last hour; and as you have heard that the antichrist is coming, even now many antichrists have come...They went out from us, but they did not really belong to us. For if they had belonged to us, they would have remained with us; but their going showed that none of them belonged to us...but **every spirit that does not acknowledge Jesus** is not from God. This is the **spirit of the antichrist**"*(1 John 2:18,19; 4:3, emphasis added).

> *"As it is written:'God gave them a **spirit of stupor,** eyes so that they could not see and ears so that they could not hear, to this very day'"* (Romans 11:8, emphasis added).

> *"And when he had called unto him his twelve disciples, he gave them power against **unclean** [foul, lewd] **spirits**"* (Matthew 10:1, KJV, emphasis added).

> *"The Lord has mingled within her a **spirit of confusion;** and they have made Egypt stagger in all her doings as a drunken man staggers in his vomit"* (Isaiah 19:14, RSV, emphasis added).

I first became acquainted with strongholds and their influence in people's lives while we were administrating a church retreat center in Connecticut from 1983 to 1993. During a conference held on Long Island in the summer of 1989, a prophecy was given to the denominationally diverse participants concerning southern New England. The prophecy stated, *"God was looking for a faceless people who were humble, with only the face of Jesus shining through. On November 30, 1989, the Lord was going to use these people in something special He was about to do."* Throughout the fall of 1989 I was haunted by the question, "Was *I* humble and faceless — would *I* be one of those the Lord was going to use?"

As I read my Bible on the morning of November 29, 1989, one day before the prophesied date, I pondered Paul's prayer for the Ephesians (3:16-19), "*I pray that out of his glorious riches he may strengthen you with power through his Spirit in your inner being, so that Christ may dwell in your hearts through faith. And I pray that you, being rooted and established in love, may have power, together with all the saints, to grasp **how wide and long and high and deep is the love of Christ, and to know this love that surpasses knowledge** — that you may be filled to the measure of all the fullness of God*" (emphasis added).

As I sat there quietly in my recliner, I was convicted that the amount of the love of Jesus that I had ever felt, even after many years in ministry, was about the size of a decimal point. The love I had perceived had no depth, breadth, or width to it, and it certainly did not surpass my knowledge. Later that day I was playing golf with my close friend Casey. As we walked along the course I shared with him my deep conviction from my reading in Ephesians that morning. I told him with determination, "I am not going on in ministry until I feel this height, depth, and breadth of the love of Jesus." He joined with me in prayer right where we stood.

The next morning at 8:00 on November 30, 1989, I received a phone call from a pastor who lived about an hour away from us. In a somewhat irritated tone he began, "Mike, what's your problem? God woke me up at 4:00 this morning and told me to call you at 8:00 AM to tell you that He had heard your prayer." When I explained to him my prayer on the golf course the day before, we both sensed that this was the reason the Lord had awakened him earlier. I continued in my ministry, waiting for God to show me the next step.

I expected God to act quickly. However, a few months went by and, in February, 1990, I received a letter from my friend Karl in Washington State. He wrote that God had shown him in prayer that our ministry was being hindered by a spirit of deceit. Sue and I prayed, but had no discernment that he was right. Several more months went by. Another friend, Mark, kept recommending a book entitled *The Three Battlegrounds* by Francis Frangipane. I purchased the book and as I reclined with it in the solitude of my study, my eyes fell upon these words: "Once a person is deceived, **he does not recognize** that he is deceived, **because he has been deceived!**"

As I pondered those words I could hear the Holy Spirit say, "Mike, you do have a spirit of deceit. Now renounce it in the name of Jesus." As I began to pray, a vision appeared in the room right in front of me. Visions are not an everyday occurrence with me. I believe God permitted me to have this vision because of the importance of the matter, not only in my own life but in the lives of others I would help through this new awareness. When God wanted Peter to minister to Cornelius, a Gentile, He gave Peter a vision to undergird the importance of the change he must undergo as a devout Jew to be willing to minister to a Gentile: "*He* [Peter] *saw heaven opened and something like a large sheet being let down to earth by its four corners. It contained all kinds of four-footed animals, as well as reptiles of the earth and birds of the air. Then a voice told him, 'Get up, Peter. Kill and eat'*" (Acts 10:11-13).

The vision appeared as an object that looked like a big black rock about five feet high and five feet wide. On it was written the word "DECEIT." As I prayed, renouncing the spirit of deceit, a veneer like an onion skin fell off the object. Underneath this veneer was the word "REJECTION." As I stared at it, God began to show me painful memories of my childhood — many of which I had forgotten. As I watched the scenes unfold, a growing sense of humiliation welled up inside me. Then the Holy Spirit revealed, "Those feelings of humiliation laid the foundation for the stronghold of rejection to be built in you. Now renounce that spirit's influence in your life." As I renounced the spirit of rejection in the name of Jesus, the black object disappeared. I was changed, but I was uncertain in what way.

The day after my vision and subsequent deliverance from the spirits of deceit and rejection, I participated in a very difficult meeting with a group of church leaders. Their denomination was in the process of introducing some very unbiblical teachings, and the men were yielding to the pressure. As I encouraged them to not give in but to uphold God's Word at all cost, they became extremely antagonistic toward me. It was at that moment that **I realized that I loved them *despite* their reaction to me. I realized that without the spirit of rejection influencing me, I was able to love them, rather than to respond negatively to them.**

As time went on, I was able to see how **the spirit of deceit had kept me from seeing things clearly**. Karl's words about deceit now made sense. Up until the time of my deliverance from these spirits, I had always painted a rosy picture of my upbringing. I had believed and convinced many others that my home was like Ozzie and Harriet's. In order to hide these feelings of humiliation, a spirit of deceit had taken over and inclined me to deny the reality of my past. (Just a note: Before the removal of the spirit of rejection, my lifetime blood pressure had been 120/90. It immediately dropped to 106/72. The tension that had been caused by the symptoms of rejection was gone!)

Months later I showed my mom the list of spiritual strongholds found in chapter 4. She immediately pointed to the stronghold of rejection and said, "This is the one I have. As a matter of fact our whole family has it." Her words began the process of breaking the influence of the spirit that has burdened our family for generations. Through what we have learned and experienced, we have been able to help many break the demonic enslavement of strongholds. This book is written to help you demolish the strongholds in your life and in your family. We welcome testimonies, input, corrections, and correspondence as you work through this material so that we may be better equipped to serve others through it. May you rejoice and give glory to God as you are set free!

Mike Dowgiewicz
Alpharetta, Georgia

"So if the Son sets you free, you will be free indeed"
(John 8:36).

Chapter 1

Creation: God Created Us with Seven Needs
(Genesis 1 and 2)

A study of the first two chapters of Genesis reveals that from the beginning God created in us **seven distinct needs.** These needs provide continuing opportunities for His people to pursue a wholehearted and intimate relationship with Him as they depend on Him to meet their needs. As we seek to meet these needs **within God's framework** revealed in His Word, we provide the spiritual environment for an ever-increasing **conformity to the image of Christ.** As we yield our **self-sufficiency** to Him and focus instead on a **God-dependency** for all our needs, we will develop spiritual eyes to see His provisions and spiritual ears to hear Him say, *"This is the way. Walk in it"* (Isaiah 30:21). When we strive to meet these needs in a way that **seems** right to our mind, will, and emotions but is not, in fact, God's way, we will suffer consequences.

> *"And my God will meet all your needs according to his glorious riches in Christ Jesus"* (Philippians 4:19).

God created us with seven needs:
Dignity
Authority
Blessing & Provision
Security
Purpose & Meaning
Freedom & Boundary
Intimate Love & Companionship
All strongholds that are built in our lives are a result of seeking to meet one or more of these needs *apart* from God's will for us.

Dignity

1. God Created Us with a Need for Dignity
"Then God said, 'Let us make man in our image, in our likeness,' ...So God created man in his own image, in the image of God he created him; male and female he created them" (Genesis 1:26,27).

The dignity of being made in the image of God elevates us above all other forms of life in creation. Dignity encompasses our sense of honor, self-respect, and our personal distinctiveness. Satan assaults our dignity because we are *temples of the Holy Spirit* (see 1 Corinthians 3:16) and *members of Christ* (see 1 Corinthians 6:15). Our bodies in God's hands are *weapons of righteousness* (see 2 Corinthians 6:7).

Dignity is often eroded in families who use **guilt as a motivator** to control behavior. Phrases such as "You didn't come to see me yesterday because I'm not important to you" or "If you loved me you would...." are manipulative and controlling. These words do not appeal to the dignity of the person or to his or her free will to act, but seek to **dominate by externally inflicted guilt**. The loss of personal dignity prevents us from understanding who we really are. We fail to develop our own unique identity. Instead, many of our actions are controlled by **what we perceive other people think of us or want from us**. Self worth and respect are difficult to maintain in this type of captivity.

- As you examine your inner person, can you discern any ongoing area where your sense of dignity is being (or has been) violated, thus discoloring your sense of acceptance by God? Are you in the habit of violating the dignity of others?

  _____

  _____

  _____

*If your sense of dignity has been violated, you may respond to those around you through a **stronghold of insecurity inhabited by a spirit of fear**. Feelings of inadequacy and inferiority may cause you to develop relationships that could lead you into activities outside the will of God because you want so desperately to be accepted.*

Authority

2. God Created Us with a Need for Authority

"And let them rule over the fish of the sea and the birds of the air, over the livestock, over all the earth, and over all the creatures that move along the ground" (Genesis 1:26).

The sense of authority and the understanding of authority have dramatic effects in our lives. Authority is the **power of position**. It is the **right to rule and influence**. The Bible tells us that authority was established by God for praise or punishment (see 1 Peter 2:14). It also states in Romans 13:1,2, *"The authorities that exist have been established by God. Consequently, **he who rebels against the authority is rebelling against what God has instituted**, and those who do so will bring judgment on themselves"* (emphasis added).

Satan uses a misunderstanding of the biblical importance of authority to bring trouble on people. He knows that **if we have trouble with authority, we have trouble with God.** It is important for us to separate a person's authority **position** (i.e. father, mother, boss) from his or her **personality and actions** in that position. We should always give deference, that is, respectfully yield to the position of our authority person or intentionally limit our choices of action or decision so that we do not provoke that person. David showed deference to King Saul even though Saul tried repeatedly to kill him (see 1 Samuel 24:1-7). Jesus recognized in the centurion such deference to authority that He could say about him, *"I have not found anyone in Israel with such great faith"* (see Matthew 8:5-13).

During retreats at the center we administrated, fathers would occasionally bring up difficulties they were having with "rebellious" children. When we asked these fathers if they themselves had slandered or gossiped about their bosses at work, many confessed that they had. We explained to them that such comments were rebellious and insubordinate against those God had placed over them. These men were reaping the consequences of the **spirit of rebellion** in their own homes. When the slanderers later asked forgiveness from their superiors for such attitudes and actions, the difficulties at home that these people had encountered also ceased.

- What response comes to mind when you think about the word "authority"? Is there a particular person your mind connects to that word? Can you think of anyone God has placed in authority over you against whom you consciously rebel?

  _____

  _____

  _____

- Are you a person who is equally as comfortable with "having authority" as with "being under authority"? Do you have a preference?

  _____

  _____

  _____

*If you find that a stubborn self-will or a certain unteachability characterizes your response to the authority figures in your life, you may have built a **stronghold of rebellion** housing a spirit that is **influencing you to defy that individual.** You are unable to see God's good purposes intended for you by using these authorities to mold yielded submission into your character.*

Blessing and Provision

3. God Created Us with a Need for Blessing and Provision

"God blessed them and said to them, 'Be fruitful and increase in number; fill the earth and subdue it. Rule over the fish of the sea and the birds of the air and over every living creature that moves on the ground.' Then God said, 'I give you every seed-bearing plant on the face of the whole earth and every tree that has fruit with seed in it. They will be yours for food'" (Genesis 1:28,29).

God's character is behind blessing and provision. His name, *Jehovah Jireh* — **God the Provider** — is key to understanding the importance of trusting Him in this area. During your upbringing, if your real or perceived needs remained unmet, then your view of God as the Provider may have been hindered. For instance, while at the retreat center we would often ask people who were worrying about money, "Did it ever occur to you that if you are prone to worry about finances, then God may bring you reason to worry just so that you may learn to repent of it and trust Him? **Your worry insults His character** — *Jehovah Jireh* — God the Provider."

Proverbs 10:3 tells us, *"The Lord does not let the righteous go hungry but he thwarts the craving of the wicked."* A **stronghold of doubt and unbelief** may characterize this sphere of your relationship with God. Renewal of trust and belief comes only upon confession and repentance of these breaches of intimacy with Him. You must demolish the stronghold by renouncing the lying spirit and allowing the work of the Holy Spirit to be released.

- On a scale of 1 to 10, where would you rate yourself in agreement with Paul's words: *"I know what it is to be in need, and I know what it is to have plenty. **I have learned the secret of being content** in any and every situation, whether well fed or hungry, whether living in plenty or in want"* (Philippians 4:12, emphasis added).

_____

_____

_____

*If you have difficulty finding contentment within the circumstances God has placed you or are fearful of a new direction to which He may be calling you (because you aren't sure the finances will be there), consider that **strongholds of fear and insecurity** may be blocking this area of your life.*

Paul says, *"I have learned to be content **whatever the circumstances**"* (Philippians 4:11, emphasis added). He tells his spiritual son Timothy, *"Godliness **with contentment** is great gain. For we brought nothing into the world, and we can take nothing out of it. But if we have food and clothing, we will **be content with that**. People who want to get rich fall into temptation and a trap and into many foolish and harmful desires that plunge men into ruin and destruction. For the love of money is a root of all kinds of evil. Some people, eager for money, have wandered from the faith and pierced themselves with many griefs"* (1 Timothy 6:6-10, emphasis added).

Paul then concludes his discussion on money and the importance of trusting God: *"Command those who are rich in this present world not to be arrogant nor to put their hope in wealth, which is so uncertain, but to **put their hope in God,** who richly provides us with everything for our enjoyment. Command them to **do good, to be rich*** *in good deeds, and to be generous and willing to share. In this way they will lay up treasure for themselves as a firm foundation for the coming age, so that they may take hold of the life that is truly life"* (1 Timothy 6:17-19, emphasis added).

Give yourself a "contentment check": Have the besetting anxieties that plague you been due to your own foolish attempts to please yourself and your family **outside of God's will for you?** Have the pressures of peer comparison, pride of life, and lust of the eyes blinded you to the **peace and acceptance with joy** that contentment with God's provision brings?

Security

4. God Created Us with a Need for Security

> *"Now the Lord God had planted a garden in the east, in Eden; and there he put the man he had formed. And the Lord God made all kinds of trees grow out of the ground — trees that were pleasing to the eye and good for food. In the middle of the garden were the tree of life and the tree of the knowledge of good and evil"* (Genesis 2:8,9).

Security may be defined as the condition in which we have confidence that we will experience **protection and relational warmth.** Spirits of **insecurity, rejection, and fear** oppress those who have grown up in homes with addictive or compulsive behavior or where some unexpected catastrophe occurred, such as the premature loss of a loved one or the sudden loss of financial security.

The absence of security leaves people in a prison, a concentration camp if you will, for years. They never seem to be able to draw close to other people in such a way that they feel like they "belong." Even in their relationship with God they never feel like He can accept them unless they are "doing something for Him." These people often hide behind conscientious behavior. They are viewed as the "reliable" ones we can trust to complete the tasks. What most are unaware of is that these people are often "driven" by the **need to be accepted or to be successful.** There is normally a tremendous "fear of failure" behind their actions.

- Can you name three people to whom you would turn in a time of desperate need? Please list them. Have you actually turned to them? When was the last time you did?

  _____

  _____

  _____

*Part of the dimension of belonging to the "body" of Christ includes **intimate interaction and relationship with other body members.** God has not called us to be "Lone Ranger" Christians!*

- List all of the activities, committees, organizations in which you are involved. Circle the ones you **know** God has called you to. Underline the ones in which you are involved for **other motives**. Are you feeling time-pressured?

_____

_____

_____

_____

_____

_____

*Once you see on paper the number of activities in which you are involved, you can begin to understand why time seems so elusive and fleeting. If you dig deeper into your soul, you might find that there is **a need you have been trying to fill by so much involvement.***

Purpose and Meaning

5. God Created Us with a Need for Purpose and Meaning

"The Lord God took the man and put him in the Garden of Eden to work it and take care of it. ...Now the Lord God had formed out of the ground all the beasts of the field and all the birds of the air. He brought them to the man to see what he would name them; and whatever the man called each living creature, that was its name" (Genesis 2:15,19).

God gave Adam work to do before the fall (yes, **before** the fall!) to endue him with purpose and meaning. The Hebrew word for work and worship is the same: *avodah.* The culture of the United States has been heavily influenced by the philosophy of the ancient Greeks who considered pleasure and self-achievement to be mankind's highest goal. The Bible represents the God-centered view of **man's highest goal,** which is captured in Deuteronomy 6:5 and repeated by our Lord Jesus Christ: "***Love the Lord your God*** *with all your heart and with all your soul and with all your mind and with all your strength"* (Mark 12:30, emphasis added).

Paul repeats the essence of the greatest of commandments so that our purpose and meaning in life would serve God's will: *"Whatever you do, **work at it with all your heart, as working for the Lord,** not for men, since you know that you will receive an inheritance from the Lord as a reward. It is the Lord Christ you are serving"* (Colossians 3:23,24, emphasis added).

Many today have lost the joy of God's purpose and meaning for their lives. Shopping malls are full of people purchasing aimlessly — believing the lie that acquisitions will bring them joy. Many labor at jobs only for material gain; they **fail**

to discern God's deeper purpose for giving them that particular job. In all our actions, we should agree with Paul's exhortation: *"And **whatever you do,** whether in word or deed, **do it all in the name of the Lord Jesus,** giving thanks to God the Father through him"* (Colossians 3:17, emphasis added). If we can't agree with this, we are lacking God's purpose and meaning for our lives.

- Can you put into words from your heart what you truly believe is the purpose and meaning for your life at this point in time?

_____

_____

_____

_____

_____

_____

*Don't despair if you can't. Recognize that God does have a significant purpose for you in His Kingdom, in order for you to **bear much fruit** and show yourself to **be His disciple,** to His Father's glory. (See John 15:8.) There may be some spiritual stronghold that is preventing you from discerning it. This is an opportunity for a few close friends to pray and fast with you, to discover both the blockage and the purpose.*

- What level of satisfaction are you finding in what you are doing at home? At work? In your faith community? In your world at large?

_____

_____

_____

*Consider the fruit of the Holy Spirit — love, joy, peace, patience, kindness, goodness, faithfulness, gentleness, self-control — as **evidence** that you have indeed discovered God's purpose and meaning for you at this time in your life!*

Freedom and Boundary

6. God Created Us with a Need for Freedom and Boundary

"And the Lord God commanded the man, 'You are free to eat from any tree in the garden; but you must not eat from the tree of the knowledge of good and evil, for when you eat of it you will surely die'" (Genesis 2:16,17).

Years ago while Mike was still in the Navy, we directed a church youth group at the base where we were stationed. At the end of the Wednesday night meetings that met in our home, some of the kids would go straight home, as their parents had requested. Others would go down to the base canteen to get an ice cream or soda. After a few months one of the young men whose parents insisted he come home immediately after the meeting said to those who were heading off to the canteen, "I envy you guys. You get to go have fun and I have to go home. I wish my parents weren't so strict." One of those heading off to the canteen responded, "Don't envy us. **Your parents love you. That's why they have you go home. Our parents don't care about us. I wish I had your Mom and Dad."**

God loved Adam and Eve; He gave them freedom and boundary **because He loved them.** We in North America have come to perceive any restraint upon our personal freedom as something negative. Many Americans consider people to be basically good, yet the Bible presents a different view concerning the basic nature of man: "*The Lord saw how great man's wickedness on the earth had become, and that every inclination of the thoughts of his heart was **only evil all the time***" (Genesis 6:5, emphasis added).

The Lord Jesus confirmed the nature of the inner man: "*But the things that come out of the mouth **come from the heart**, and these make man 'unclean'. For **out of the heart** come evil thoughts, murder, adultery, sexual immorality, theft, false testimony, slander. These are what make a man 'unclean'*" (Matthew 15:18-20, emphasis added).

Because the basic nature of man is to do evil, the Bible tells parents to "***Impress them*** [the commands of God] *on your children. **Talk about them** when you sit at home and when you walk along the road, when you lie down and when you get up*" (Deuteronomy 6:7, emphasis added). "*He who spares the rod hates his son, but he who loves him is **careful to discipline him**.*" (Proverbs 13:24, emphasis added). "*Folly is bound up in the heart of a child, but the **rod of discipline** will drive it far from him*" (Proverbs 22:15, emphasis added). We have been created with a need for the **boundaries that God has established in His Word.** Failure to be diligent in having His commandments instilled in our children may cause them to probe the arena of sin to seek fulfillment.

- Against what boundaries — restraints on your personal freedom — do you find yourself tempted to push a little too hard?

  _____

  _____

  _____

Ask yourself why you may be testing your limits. **Spirits of bitterness, control, or idolatry** *could be influencing your desire to stray from God's will for you.*

Intimate Love and Companionship

7. God Created Us to Experience Intimate Love and Companionship

"The Lord God said, 'It is not good for the man to be alone. I will make a helper suitable for him'" (Genesis 2:18). *"For Adam no suitable helper was found. So the Lord God caused the man to fall into a deep sleep; and while he was sleeping, he took one of the man's ribs and closed up the place with flesh. Then the Lord God made a woman from the rib he had taken out of the man, and he brought her to the man. The man said, 'This is now bone of my bones and flesh of my flesh; she shall be called "woman", for she was taken out of man.' For this reason a man will leave his father and mother and be united to his wife, and they will become one flesh. The man and his wife were both naked, and they felt no shame"* (Genesis 2:20-25).

> **Consider this:**
> Over 70 percent of all weddings in the U. S. are performed in church buildings — and nearly 50 percent of these end in divorce.

It's amazing just how many of the people we have ministered to over the years yearn for intimate love and companionship! Satan has exhibited such great triumph over us by robbing us of our ability to experience loving and intimate relationships **God's way.** Many marriages are hollow. Sexual relationships have been based more on the teachings of Hugh Hefner and other pornographers than on the beauty that Adam and Eve experienced.

"Intimate love and companionship" implies the need to be **loved, understood, and accepted.** How many times is 1 Corinthians 13 read at weddings and yet the fruit of love diminishes rather than grows over the years of the marriage?

The **stronghold of fear** and the accompanying symptoms that the spirit therein induces restrict our ability to love and to feel the love of others, including the love of God. As strongholds are demolished and the **presence of Jesus** is allowed to fill those areas of our soul, **love replaces fear.** *"God is love. Whoever lives in love lives in God, and God in him. In this way, love is made complete among us so that we will have confidence on the day of judgment, because in this world we are like him. There is no fear in love. But perfect love drives out fear, because fear has to do with punishment. The one who fears is not made perfect in love"* (1 John 4:16-18).

As we seek love "in all the wrong places," Satan's servants deceive us into rationalizing that we **have a right** to loving companionship **outside of God's will.** Each failed relationship further diminishes our trust level, thus filling us with cynicism and hopelessness in this area of our lives.

- How would you describe your relationship with your spouse or most intimate friend(s)? Deepening steadily? Staying pretty much the same? Heading downhill?

_____

_____

_____

*As we grow in the **sacrificial love** that exemplifies a Christ-like character, our relationships also deepen and strengthen.*

- Describe a point in your life when you experienced a relationship that you wished would never change. What happened to change it?

_____

_____

_____

Our lives are not static. The dynamics of daily life cause circumstances and relationships to change for either better or worse. We must discern through the Holy Spirit how to respond to these changes.

Our life is a pilgrimage — a journey during which changing circumstances force us to adapt.

Our ability to make those adaptations in the power of the Holy Spirit will determine the level of joy and peace we find in our relationship with God and with others.

Our victory of walking in the fullness of Christ will not be achieved until we meet the needs God has created in us, in the manner that He prescribes.

Chapter 2

The Demonic Forces In Strongholds

In the New Testament, those who are afflicted by evil spirits are often said to be "demon-possessed." The Greek word translated in these instances, *daimonizomenoi,* is more literally rendered "**demonized**," that is, **afflicted or influenced in some degree by demons.** The emphasis is more on **degrees of influence** than on total possession. The intensity of demonization varies, as seen in the deranged man from the region of the Gerasenes who was inhabited by *a legion of evil spirits* (see Mark 5:1-20); the young man thrown into convulsions by *the spirit* tormenting him (see Luke 9:38-43); the *demonized* man who cried out in the synagogue where Jesus was teaching, *"What do you want with us, Jesus of Nazareth? Have you come to destroy us?"* (see Luke 4:33-36); and the slave girl who had *a spirit* by which she predicted the future (see Acts 16:16).

As believers in Christ, we have been marked by the seal of the Holy Spirit, *"A deposit guaranteeing our inheritance until the redemption of those who are God's possession"* (Ephesians 1:14). We are owned by God; yet to the extent in which we have **fellowship with demons** (Greek *koinonia* in 1 Corinthians 10:20) we open ourselves to demonic influence and affliction **by our choices to sin.**

The battlefield for believers exists in our **mind, will, and emotions** — what we often refer to as the **soul**. It is here that we face our daily decisions of Spirit-controlled living or sin-influenced living: *"Those who live according to the sinful nature have their **minds set** on what that nature desires; but those who live in accordance with the Spirit have their **minds set** on what the Spirit desires. The **mind of sinful man** is death, but the **mind controlled by the Spirit** is life and peace; the **sinful mind** is hostile to God. It does not submit to God's law, nor can it do so"* (Romans 8:5-7, emphasis added).

Note the following warnings given to BELIEVERS — because we ARE susceptible to demonic attack, these admonitions are absolutely necessary.

- *"Put on the full armor of God so that you can **take your stand against the devil's schemes**"* (Ephesians 6:11, emphasis added).

- *"For **our struggle** is not against flesh and blood, but against the rulers, against the authorities, against the powers of this dark world and against the **spiritual forces of evil** in the heavenly realms"* (Ephesians 6:12, emphasis added).

- *"Be self-controlled and alert. Your enemy the devil prowls around like a roaring lion **looking for someone to devour**"* (1 Peter 5:8, emphasis added).

- *"He [Satan] was given power to **make war against the saints** and to conquer them"* (Revelation 13:7, emphasis added).

- *"The Spirit clearly says that in later times some will abandon the faith and **follow deceiving spirits and things taught by demons**"* (1 Timothy 4:1, emphasis added).

- *"Those who oppose him [the Lord's servant] he must gently instruct, in the hope that God will grant them repentance leading them to a knowledge of the truth, and that they will come to their senses and **escape from the trap of the devil,** who has **taken them captive to do his will**"* (2 Timothy 2:25-26, emphasis added).

- *"But I am afraid that just as Eve was deceived by the serpent's cunning, **your minds may somehow be led astray** from your sincere and pure devotion to Christ"* (2 Corinthians 11:3, emphasis added).

Key to the destruction of strongholds is 2 Corinthians 10:3-6,

"For though we live in the world, we do not wage war as the world does. The weapons we fight with are not the weapons of the world. On the contrary, they have divine power to demolish strongholds. We demolish arguments and every pretension that sets itself up against the knowledge of God, and we take captive every thought to make it obedient to Christ."

We can clearly see by these verses that we are indeed engaged in the **same manner of spiritual warfare** that Jesus and His disciples confronted. Both the Old and New Testaments are replete with references to **evil and unclean spirits** (Greek *pneuma* in the New Testament and Hebrew *ruach* in the Old Testament).

The decisions we make to give in to temptation open up a **foothold for demonic influence.** One-third of the angels sided with Satan in their rebellion against God and were cast down to the earth. While we do not know their exact number, we can surmise that there are significant quantities of them to wage war against believers. But as we will explore in the following chapters, our **weapons of warfare** in this daily struggle to **choose righteousness** rather than

succumb to temptation are indeed *"mighty through God to the pulling down of strongholds"* (2 Corinthians 10:4, KJV).

The Bible tells us that we are comprised of body, soul, and spirit: *"May God himself, the God of peace, sanctify you through and through. May your **whole spirit, soul and body** be kept blameless at the coming of our Lord Jesus Christ"* (1 Thessalonians 5:23, emphasis added). The **body** is the part that is subject to the physical frailties of injury, disease, and ultimately death. The **soul** consists of our mind, will, and emotions — the arenas of thought, determination, and feelings. The **spirit** represents the eternal part of our being owned either by Satan as the ruler of this world's system, or by God, Who has redeemed us from slavery to sin. The spiritual world is hidden from our vision, but nonetheless is **very real**. As believers we are encouraged by the assurance that our *"spirits are seated with Christ in the heavenly realms"* (Ephesians 2:6), and sealed with the indwelling Holy Spirit during our earthly pilgrimage. (See Ephesians 1:13.)

In the spiritual realm there is a tremendous battle going on for the souls of men. In effect, it is a battle of God versus Satan. Its outcome will determine whether the truth of Jesus and His Lordship will reign or the deception of Satan will triumph. [NOTE: The overwhelming evidence in the Bible shows that God's plan for our lives is to **conform us in character and power to the image of Jesus Christ.**]

According to pollster George Barna, almost half of today's Christians **discredit the reality of "the devil"** in the person of Satan. *The authors don't.* His hatred for those who love God means that we are exposed to constant conflict and temptation. **We must be on alert!**

What can you know about Satan from the following verses?

- **He Is the Ruler of the Kingdom of the Air, Now at Work in Those Who Disobey God**
  "As for you, you were dead in your transgressions and sins, in which you used to live when you followed the ways of this world and of the ruler of the kingdom of the air, the spirit who is now at work in those who are disobedient" (Ephesians 2:1,2).

- **He Masquerades As an Angel of Light**
  "And no wonder, for Satan himself masquerades as an angel of light. It is not surprising, then, if his servants masquerade as servants of righteousness" (2 Corinthians 11:14,15).

- **He Takes People Captive To Do His Will**
  "That they will come to their senses and escape the trap of the devil, who has taken them captive to do his will" (2 Timothy 2:26).

What can you know from the following verses about the battle going on over the souls of men?

- **We Are Not Fighting a Habit, a Character Weakness, Or Even Other People**
  "For our struggle is not against flesh and blood, but against the rulers, against the authorities, against the powers of this dark world and against the spiritual forces of evil in the heavenly realms" (Ephesians 6:12).

- **Satan Is Committed to Our Destruction**
  "Then the dragon [earlier described as Satan in Rev. 12:9] *was enraged at the woman and went off to make war against the rest of her offspring — those who obey God's commandments and hold to the testimony of Jesus"* (Revelation 12:17).

- **Jesus Came To Destroy the Work of Satan in Every Believer's Life**
  "He who does what is sinful is of the devil, because the devil has been sinning from the beginning. The reason the Son of God appeared was to destroy the devil's work" (1 John 3:8).

- **Satan Is Always at Work**
  "Be self-controlled and alert. Your enemy the devil prowls around like a roaring lion looking for someone to devour" (1 Peter 5:8).

Satan's influence in our lives is often hidden, controlled through **strongholds** in our soul — our mind, will, and emotions. (NOTE: In the Old Testament, the Hebrew word for **"stronghold"** is often used in a positive way to denote a fortification or defender for protection, as in 2 Samuel 22:3, *"He is my **stronghold**, my refuge and my savior"* and Psalm 144:2, *"He is my loving God and my fortress, my **stronghold** and my deliverer."* In the New Testament, however, a very different negative connotation of the "fortress" idea appears. The enemy is not kept out. The spirits of darkness have been given permission **by my sinful decisions** to take up residence within those areas of my soul **not yielded fully to Christ**. The freedom available to me in Christ is denied and I am kept imprisoned by the influence of those spirits.

The Definition of Strongholds

A **stronghold** is a **demonic fortress of thoughts housing evil spirits** that **(1) control, dictate, and influence our attitudes and behavior; (2) oppress and discourage us; (3) filter and color how we view or react to situations, circumstances, or people.** As we entertain thoughts and participate in activities that are **contrary to the will of God,** we open ourselves up to demonic inhabitation **in those areas.** When these thoughts and activities become **habitual,** we allow a **spiritual fortification** to be built around that spirit and its influence. We become so accustomed to responding to the "voice" of that spirit that its abode in us is secure.

Demons monitor our activities and set up circumstances to tempt us. They agitate our thoughts and emotions until we are too confused to remember to pray. They cause us to **misperceive situations** to the detriment of our relationships with others. Through demonic agitation we **develop wrong conclusions** to other people's actions toward us.

Many of our incorrect beliefs and attitudes have been learned through our environment, i.e., family circumstances, life and relationship experiences, and educational influences. Knowledge acquired from secular sources that disagree with biblical truth lodges doubt and unbelief into our spiritual perspective. All our thoughts can be traced back to beliefs based either on the **truth of Scripture or on Satan's lies.** Through our wrong interpretation of life situations, we establish a dwelling place for satanic activity in our souls.

A demonic stronghold is anything compelling enough to hold you in its power to **keep you from receiving God's love and truth.** With a stronghold built in you, that spirit arouses a defensive posture that causes you to "**rationalize**" your current situation. The existence of a stronghold can be recognized because it will be that area of your life in which you **consistently have problems** and **cannot live in victory.** You can tell one is established because a **habitual pattern** of failure or hopelessness exists.

Our world view — our personal perspective of reality — colors all our decision making. This perspective has developed over a long period, including the time before we became Christians. Many of our innate responses to situations are rooted in the character of Satan, the father of lies. He guides our wrong emotional responses to the circumstances we face. The circumstance itself does not cause the emotion, but **what we believe** about the circumstance does.

The Process of Stronghold Development

Strongholds are developed through **demonic agitation.** For example, reflect on some **thought** that you realize in your spirit is contrary to the mind of Christ, such as a sexual fantasy. At this point you have two options: 1) You can rebuke the spirit that put the thought there and think on those things that are "*true, noble, right, pure, lovely, admirable, excellent or praiseworthy,*" as Paul recommends in Philippians 4:8. Or, 2) You can entertain that thought a little longer. At this point you begin to **develop an emotion** about that thought — lust, arousal, fantasy. As that emotion continues, you are moved to **take some action,** if not now, then at some ripe moment in the future. The seed of fantasy will eventually grow into an opportunity to fulfill that emotional longing, and a sexual enactment may follow. If you choose to ignore the warning convictions of the Holy Spirit, you will continue in these actions until they become **habitual.** At that point, without God's power released in you by your repentance, you are then held prisoner to this habit by a spirit — a **spiritual stronghold** has been built in you. The "voice" of that spirit sounds just like your own inner voice; you don't detect its presence.

> *In Summary*
> 1) *Satanic-inspired **THOUGHTS** are introduced into my mind.*
> 2) *Entertaining these thoughts brings on **EMOTIONS.***
> 3) *Giving in to emotions eventually leads to taking some sort of **ACTION.***
> 4) *Continual participation in this behavior causes me to develop a **HABIT.***
> 5) *Once a habit is developed, a **STRONGHOLD** is built by that spirit.*

How Does God Get Shut Out?

Since the "*Spirit of him who raised Jesus from the dead is living in* [us]" (Romans 8:11), we have the power to **conform our minds** to that of Jesus. We are able to **make decisions** that are pleasing to God according to the truth of His Word. The weapons we use to wage war against the forces of darkness "*have divine power to demolish strongholds. We demolish arguments and every pretension that sets itself up against the knowledge of God*" (2 Corinthians 10:4,5). We can elect to put our feelings under the **control of the Holy Spirit.**

But once our souls are infiltrated by a stronghold, our mind, will, and emotions filter all our perceptions through that demonic stronghold. This does not mean we are "demon-possessed"; we are "demonized" in those areas habitually given over to sin. As followers of Christ, we are inhabited by the Holy Spirit. However, those areas that we have **willingly yielded to sin** are fair game to become **footholds for satanic involvement.** We are warned in Luke 11:35,36, "***See to it, then, that the light within you is not darkness.*** *Therefore, if your whole body is full of light, and no part of it dark, it will be completely lighted, as when the light of a lamp shines on you*" (emphasis added).

Note the differences between arguments and pretensions.

ARGUMENTS: "Reasoning, rationalizations, vain imaginations." This part of a stronghold concerns the **thought processes** and patterns we use to **deny that there is a problem.** When we raise these arguments like walls, as in the diagram that follows, **God's Love and His Truths are prevented** from entering our thoughts. Our **rationalizations and justifications** for our attitudes and behaviors keep the humility that precedes repentance from seizing our hearts and convicting us of sin.

PRETENSIONS: "Boastful; false appearance designed to deceive." This part of the stronghold reveals the **pride and rebellion** that we raise like another wall to **prevent us from seeking the power of the Holy Spirit** in personal prayer or through ministry to release us from captivity. Again, the **Love and Truths of God are blocked** from penetrating our decision-making processes.

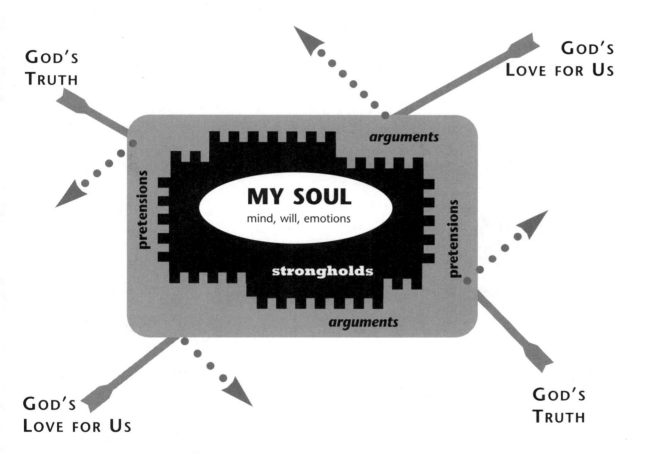

Some area of our mind, will, and emotions shown in the diagram above has continued in **sinful defiance of God's will** through the influence of a spirit or spirits. All other activities and relationships are filtered through the thoughts, decisions, and feelings aroused and agitated by the spirit that is protected by the stronghold "fortress." We are probably unaware that these thoughts and feelings are being whispered to us because the "voice" sounds **just like our own internal voice.** When confronted with opposition to our decisions or actions, we **deny** that we have a problem **(argument)** or rationalize that we **have a right** to the emotion or activity that we are pursuing **(pretension).** The convicting work of the Holy Spirit that would otherwise cause us to repent and confess our rebellion to God's ways and truth **is blocked out.** He is faithfully presenting the truth to us out of His great love, but we have chosen by habitual pattern to heed the familiar voice of the demonic spirit protected in its stronghold.

Another way of understanding the effects of strongholds can be seen in the next diagram. Key to grasping this concept is 1 Corinthians 2:13,14: *"This is what we speak, **not in words taught us by human wisdom but in words taught by the Spirit,** expressing spiritual truths in spiritual words. The man without the Spirit does not accept the things that come from the Spirit of God, for they are foolishness to him, and he cannot understand them, because they are spiritually discerned"* (emphasis added).

Here is an example of how this plays itself out when strongholds exist.

Person #1 is a pastor seeking a message for his congregation. The Holy Spirit gives him a message to share that **passes into his soul through his spirit.** As he preaches his message, the words pass out of his body through his mouth and enter the body of Person #2 through his ears and thus **into his mind, will, and emotions.** He may hear the words but **fail to understand the spiritual truths** and the

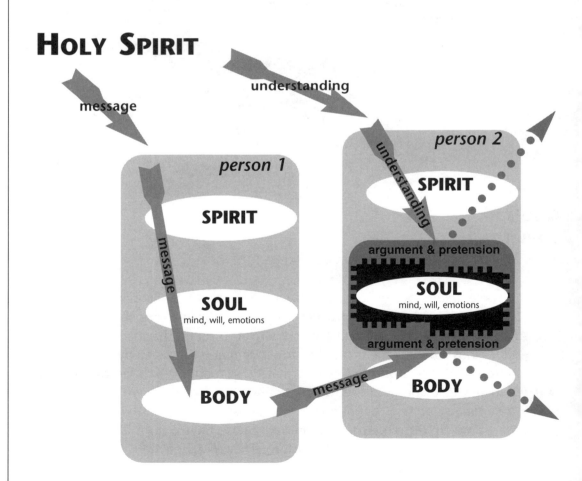

application of those truths. (We see this so often when asking church attendees, "What was the sermon about this past Sunday?" They can't even remember the main point of the message.) Because the truths are from the Holy Spirit and are **"spiritually discerned,"** the Holy Spirit in Person #2 would have affirmed, strengthened, and brought into application the truth that was spoken and heard **if the arguments and pretensions of the strongholds had not blocked** the empowerment of the Spirit to do this.

Many of God's children crave to hear His voice and feel His love but they are hindered because of the interference of strongholds. Even as the Holy Spirit seeks to bring a certain area of our lives into submission to God's will, the arguments and pretensions associated with the strongholds **ward off the truth of God's love;** there is now a breach in our fellowship with God. We cannot clearly hear His will for our lives with a pure heart; a sinful blockage deafens our will to obey and impairs our intimacy with the Father.

Thoughts to consider concerning strongholds

- Think of a situation in which you totally misperceived the motivation or intent of a person close to you. How did that misperception affect your relationship with that person?

  _____

  _____

  _____

  *If you have never felt accepted or valued as a worthwhile individual, you might suspect that your friend was only trying to benefit himself or herself. The **stronghold of rejection** may be manifested as a spirit arouses unwarranted suspicion or even withdrawal from your friend.*

- How did you feel when you realized that you had wrongly interpreted that person's intent or actions?

  _____

  _____

  _____

  *You may have felt tremendous guilt or a sense of unworthiness. The **stronghold of rejection** might cause you to believe that you don't deserve friends because you are such a poor one yourself.*

- How did you handle the relational breach? Did you find it difficult to humbly confess and ask forgiveness? Did you prefer to sweep it under the carpet as though nothing had happened? Did you feel pressure to rationalize and blame the other person?

_____

_____

_____

*The spirit in a **stronghold of rejection** could escalate your embarrassment and guilt to such an extent that it might prevent you from seeking forgiveness for your response. You might also choose to ignore the situation out of fear that your friend would be angry and reject you completely.*

Another example: What if the mental framework of your childhood focused on the memory that your father often disciplined you harshly? Every time you have thought about yourself and your father, you have had difficulty remembering happy times of togetherness because that one painful perception has filtered them out. Suppose you discovered that, in fact, the discipline situation actually occurred **only once**, but you were so humiliated by it that you then allowed the **lie** of "frequent disciplining" to replace the **truth** of "one severe disciplining"? You are being "held captive" by the **spirits of bitterness and anger** that have induced you to believe Satan's lies. Until you **root out** your false beliefs about the circumstances that framed those beliefs and **replace** them with the truth found in Jesus and His Word, you will never change; you will remain a **prisoner**, captive to the spirits in the stronghold(s). Until truth replaces the rationalizations of the lie, you will be prevented from experiencing freedom in expressing the life of Christ in your inner being. God's grace and abundance will be deflected from affecting that area of your life.

Chapter 3

How Adam's Fall into Sin Has Harmed Us
(Genesis 3:1-4:7)

The following examination of Genesis 3 provides a parallel of how Satan (the serpent) deceived Adam and Eve and, through demonic strongholds, **continues to deceive us today.**

A Stronghold

1. Harms Our Hearing from God

> *"Now the serpent was more crafty than any of the wild animals the Lord God had made. He said to the woman, '**Did God really say,** "You must not eat from any tree in the garden"?' The woman said to the serpent, 'We may eat fruit from the trees in the garden, but God did say, "You must not eat fruit from the tree that is in the middle of the garden, and **you must not touch it,** or you will die"'"* (Genesis 3:1-3, emphasis added).

If we allow our sinful thoughts to lead to habitual sinful actions that lay the foundation for strongholds in our souls, we lose connection with the Source of truth. In the Greek language, *truth* and *reality* are the same word. The Lord affirmed the understanding that He was the only reality when He said: *"I am the way and the truth* [reality] *and the life. No one comes to the Father except through me"* (John 14:6). Anything that is **not** truth — **not of Jesus, therefore** — alters our reality into some sort of lie.

- Do you find yourself thinking that the Bible is "culturally entrapped" — that the timeless truths of God somehow don't apply to your current situation? What answer would you give to someone who presented that argument to you?

_____

_____

_____

*Any time we try to **rationalize** an attitude or behavior that deviates from God's commands expressed in the Bible, we are **opening a foothold** for the enemy to plant seeds of distrust in the Author of the Word. It behooves us to become faithful students of the Word so that we might discern the life choices that will bring glory to God through us.*

- How might a stronghold of insecurity affect your trust in the heavenly Father Who has promised to meet all your needs according to His glorious riches in Christ Jesus? (See Philippians 4:19.)

_____

_____

_____

*God is infinitely creative in the means by which He keeps His promises. If we pray for specific answers to our problems, rather than presenting to God our petitions and requests with thanksgiving, we may not even recognize the provision from His hand when it appears. We may doubt He even heard us. In this way, **a stronghold will hinder our hearing from God.***

2. Harms Our Belief in God

*"'**You will not surely die**,'" the serpent said to the woman. 'For God knows that when you eat of it your eyes will be opened, and **you will be like God**, knowing good and evil'"* (Genesis 3:4,5, emphasis added).

The framework of our faith requires us to *"trust in the Lord with all* [our] *heart and lean not on* [our] *own understanding"* (Proverbs 3:5). We cannot view God as merely a repository of holy righteousness Who is independent of our earthly struggles. Our deceitful hearts are prone to make **Him** into **our image** of **Who we think He should be.** Sin causes us to doubt, or at least to hedge on, the reality of His character as revealed in His Word. Strongholds of **deception or doubt and unbelief** replace the truth with a rationalized slant that seems logical but leads to death. (See Proverbs 14:12.)

- What areas of doubt or unbelief do you want to take up with God: Why do the innocent suffer? Why haven't my unsaved relatives yielded to You? Why is it taking so long for my prayers to be answered? Something else?

_____

_____

_____

_____

_____

God is not obligated to explain Himself to His creation. Perhaps too our finite under-standing could not even grasp the purposes of Him Whose ways are not our ways and Whose thoughts far surpass our thoughts (see Isaiah 55:8,9). **A stronghold, therefore, taints what we believe about God.**

3. Harms Our Desires

*"When the woman saw that the fruit of the tree was good for food and pleasing to the eye, and also **desirable for gaining wisdom**"* (Genesis 3:6, emphasis added).

Have you learned to be content in whatever your circumstances? Dissatisfaction, comparison, and competition are all "horizontally focused"; that is, what our eyes see in other people our minds then want, if we have not learned to desire **only what God desires for us.** This "vertical parameter" — **limiting our desires to God's will and means of provision** — is His protection for us in that area of our hearts. When strongholds of **jealousy, insecurity, and idolatry** hold us, we become distrusting of God's plans. We take matters into our own hands — agitated by the demonic spirits — and seek something we think is in our best interest but is not in God's plan for our lives. Our old nature, corrupted by its deceitful desires, again directs our will.

- How might you rationalize an action or acquisition because it "seemed right" at the time? What instance can you recall in which you just went ahead and did something because you wanted to, without seeking God's plan first?

  _____

  _____

  _____

There is much to be said for the counsel of your spouse or of a mentor whose life bespeaks faithfulness to God. Frequently they can see through your outward responses and explanations and probe your true motivations. These then can be held up to the Light of Christ for examination. **Unfortunately, strongholds distort your desires in opposition to God's will for you.**

4. Harms Our Actions

*"**She took some and ate it**"* (Genesis 3:6, emphasis added).

If you decide to dally with sinful thoughts, then sinful actions will result. If you refuse to submit to God and resist the devil, then he will be your companion in sin. A stronghold of **pride, idolatry, or sexual impurity** will influence you to pursue your own goal so wholeheartedly that any potentially negative outcomes are minimized in your mind. There are, however, **always painful consequences** to sin. The pleasure of the moment is fleeting, and the subsequent guilt and regret further remove you from the intimate companionship you once enjoyed with God. *"But each one is tempted when, by his own evil desire, he is dragged away and enticed. Then, after desire has conceived, it gives birth to sin; and sin, when it is full-grown, gives birth to death"* (James 1:14,15).

- What counsel would you give to a close friend who is contemplating an action that you know violates God's will? How would you counsel that person if he or she were right in the middle of that sinful circumstance? After he or she has decided to try to stop the sinful behavior or attitude? Have you ever been involved in a circumstance like this when you knew you should speak up?

_____

_____

_____

When the fortresses of demonic influence — strongholds — have been built in our mind, will, and emotions, our

> HEARING from God
> is altered;
> BELIEF in God
> is shaken;
> DESIRES
> are distorted;
> ACTIONS
> are disobedient;
> RELATIONSHIPS
> are debased.

*Part of being your "brother's keeper" involves **risking the friendship for his good,** especially if he is heading away from God and toward the enemy's territory. If you take a courageous yet loving stand for righteousness, your valor and words may help your friend **recognize and defeat** the stronghold that has been tempting him to sin.*

5. Harms Our Relationships with Others
*"She also gave some to **her husband, who was with her, and he ate it**"* (Genesis 3:6, emphasis added).

There is good reason for the warning in Proverbs 1:10: *"My son, if sinners entice you, do not give in to them."* A person considering sin is more likely to succumb to it if someone else joins in. We rationalize by saying, "What's **wrong** with it?" (instead of, "What's **right** with it!"). Then we try to justify the sin by thinking that if it were really so bad others would not be doing it. Note that God is entirely out of the decision loop here. A **stronghold of deceit** influences us to believe that sinful actions may even strengthen our relationships.

- Can you recall an instance when you were "sucked in" to a sinful activity at the request of someone you cared for? Did you realize at the time that you were violating God's standards? Did that realization inhibit your participation in any way? How did you feel afterward? Did you sense any separation from God or loss of intimacy with Him?

_____

_____

_____

*We know from 1 John 1:9, "If we confess our sins, he is faithful and just and will for-give us our sins and purify us from all unrighteousness." Genuine confession of our sin will bring forgiveness and cleansing. However, we also have a **responsibility** to **those with whom we have sinned.** We need to humbly seek their forgiveness for joining in the sin, and make restitution wherever appropriate.*

Further Effects of Adam's Fall

Verse after verse reiterates the reality of our sinfulness: *"There is no one righteous, not even one; there is no one who understands, no one who seeks God"* (Romans 3:10,11); *"For all have sinned and fall short of the glory of God"* (Romans 3:23); *I know that nothing good lives in me, that is, in my sinful nature. For I have the desire to do what is good, but I cannot carry it out"* (Romans 7:18). If left alone in our sin natures, the **consequence will be death.**

As with our original parents in the Garden of Eden, we too have the oppor-tunity to humble ourselves before God and confess with true repentance that through sin we have "missed the mark" of His holiness. The enemy, however, has a different plan. He activates his demonic forces to agitate us so that obedience to God's plan of forgiveness and cleansing is obscured in our minds.

Instead of receiving the forgiveness and restoration of the cross, we are tormented with the following.

1. **Shame** (Condemnation)
    *"Then the eyes of both of them were opened, and **they realized they were naked**; so they sewed fig leaves together and made coverings for themselves"* (Genesis 3:7, emphasis added).

2. **Rationalization** (Hiding from God)
    *"Then the man and his wife heard the sound of the Lord God as he was walking in the garden in the cool of the day, and **they hid from the Lord God** among the trees of the garden. But the Lord God called to the man, 'Where are you?'"* (Genesis 3:8,9, emphasis added).

3. **Fear**
    *"He answered, 'I heard you in the garden, and **I was afraid** because I was naked; so I hid'"* (Genesis 3:10, emphasis added).

4. **Blame** (Inability To Take Responsibility for One's Actions)
    *"And he said, 'Who told you that you were naked? Have you eaten from the tree that I commanded you not to eat from?' The man said, '**The woman you put here with me**—she gave me some fruit from the tree, and I ate it.' Then the Lord God said to the woman, 'What is this you have done?' The woman said, '**The serpent deceived me,** and I ate'* (Genesis 3:11-13, emphasis added).

5. Curse Instead of Blessing

"To the woman he said, 'I will greatly increase your pains in childbearing; with pain you will give birth to children. Your desire will be for your husband, and he will rule over you.' To Adam he said, 'Because you listened to your wife and ate from the tree about which I commanded you, "You must not eat of it," Cursed is the ground because of you; through painful toil you will eat of it all the days of your life. It will produce thorns and thistles for you, and you will eat the plants of the field. By the sweat of your brow you will eat your food until you return to the ground, since from it you were taken; for dust you are and to dust you will return'" (Genesis 3:16-19, emphasis added).

6. Rejection

"The Lord God made garments of skin for Adam and his wife and clothed them. And the Lord God said, 'The man has now become like one of us, knowing good and evil. He must not be allowed to reach out his hand and take also from the tree of life and eat, and live forever.' So the Lord God banished him from the Garden of Eden to work the ground from which he had been taken. After he drove the man out, he placed on the east side of the Garden of Eden cherubim and a flaming sword flashing back and forth to guard the way to the tree of life" (Genesis 3:21-24, emphasis added).

7. Vulnerability to Satanic Attack

"Then the Lord said to Cain, 'Why are you angry? Why is your face downcast? If you do what is right, will you not be accepted? But if you do not do what is right, sin is crouching at your door; it desires to have you, but you must master it'" (Genesis 4:6,7, emphasis added).

- Which of these **seven consequences of sin** most often plague you? Do you find yourself afflicted by one or more of these effects of the fall even **after** you have confessed your sin to God? Why do you suppose this happens?

_____

_____

_____

_____

_____

If you do not deal with the underlying strongholds that distort your relationship with God, you will *continue* to expose yourself to the effects of the fall. Loving intimacy with the God of Holiness will seem out of reach.

Chapter 4

Steps To Identify And Demolish Strongholds

Recall that strongholds are built when you try to meet any of the seven basic needs that God created in you by ways that are contrary to His will. You end up wounded in the process. Once you determine the nature of a particular stronghold, you must **renounce that spirit's presence and influence** in your life.

You must still **discern the need that is lacking** or unfulfilled and meet it in a way that God intended. It is important for you to be part of other caring relationships in the Body of Christ that can be used by God to meet these needs. Until this last step — meeting your needs within the will of God — is complete, you will be vulnerable to further stronghold formation.

> Members of the Body of Christ can be used by God to meet our seven needs in ways that He intended. Until we meet our needs within the will of God, the potential for strongholds to form again is very great.

REMEMBER: Once a stronghold is established, you provide a **"foothold"** for the devil (see Ephesians 4:27), a base of operations for the **"strongman"** (see Matthew 12:29). You then become vulnerable to **demonic control, direction, influence and/or oppression** (mild or heavy) in that area of your life. Not dealing with this stronghold can engender further demonic activity and lead to the establishment of other strongholds with additional demonic oppression in other areas of your life.

This chapter contains examples of strongholds **(bold type)** on page 37. Beneath each stronghold heading are listed related **thoughts, feelings, or attitudes** often produced by demonic agitation in order to sustain that stronghold. This list of strongholds shows the ones we have previously encountered. **It does not represent an exhaustive list.** God may reveal to you other strongholds and symptoms to which you have given ground. The related areas may be similar for certain strongholds, so use careful and sensitive discernment to identify the correct one. For example, one of the symptoms of the stronghold of **Bitterness** is anger. The stronghold of **Rebellion** also has the symptom of anger, but the type of anger noted here normally leads to arguments.

REMEMBER: Strongholds are demonic forces at work **influencing and controlling your soul** (i.e. your mind, will, and emotions). The most common goal of all strongholds is to **destroy relationships.** They not only block us from knowing and experiencing God's truth and love, but also prevent us from giving and receiving love, understanding, and acceptance in other relationships. Because of the nature of marriage, couples are particularly susceptible to the effects of strongholds in their relationship.

Identify the Strongholds

Through our experience, we have found it extremely valuable to **solicit the help of family members** or others with whom you have had a close relationship. The participation of others is advantageous, but if you do not have access to family members or someone else to whom you are close, the steps we suggest may be done alone. If you are married, ask your spouse to participate with you. Even the participation of teenage children has proved to be very helpful in the identification of **family strongholds.**

Our experience has shown that most strongholds have been **passed along for generations** within families. The vast majority of troubled marriages we have encountered have had the same prevailing strongholds **in both spouses,** and each spouse had received these from his or her respective parents. When the stronghold list was given out to churches, **most people in the church** had the same prevailing strongholds. When we have used it in businesses, many of the **key employees** have identified the same predominant strongholds. In effect, it is not the people but the **spirits in the strongholds** controlling the goals, methods, and values of families, churches, and businesses. (We are uncertain how this occurs, but the data are overwhelming.) Again, the symptoms may seem different on the surface, but the stronghold behind the symptoms is often the same.

> Do not be overwhelmed if you discover you have checked off a large number of strongholds. God is not condemning you. He wants you to demolish these spiritual forces by His power so that your fellowship with Him may be fully restored.

One of the methods we have found successful in identifying strongholds is to have family members or other significant person(s) check off the applicable symptoms under each stronghold that they think **pertain to you.** (This can be done to identify the strongholds that may be hidden from you, or more importantly, as a step to identify the strongholds in the family, home fellowship, church, or business.) Use a **scale from 1 to 10,** with 1 indicating low and 10 indicating high, next to each symptom to indicate the strength of its control, influence, or oppression. When others participate, you may want to have them indicate one number for you and a second number indicating the strength of the symptoms in themselves. By comparing and discussing the combined input, a more reliable picture can be obtained as to the type and intensity of stronghold. You also can determine how pervasive the influence is in the family, home fellowship, church, or business.

OVERVIEW OF TYPES OF STRONGHOLDS

(NOTE: Use worksheets on following pages to evaluate symptoms.)

DECEIT
Lying
Fantasies
Delusions
Rationalizations
Wrong doctrine/misuse
of Scripture

CONFUSION (DOUBT & UNBELIEF)
Suspicious
Apprehensive
Indecisive
Skeptical
Unsettled

INDEPENDENCE & DIVORCE
Insensitivity
Loneliness
Self-determination
Aloofness
Withdrawal
Excuse making
Lack of trust
"Martyr" complex

CONTROL
Manipulative
Striving
Lacking trust
Worried
Insensitive
Desiring recognition
Violent

BITTERNESS
Resentment
Hate
Unforgiveness
Anger
Violence
Revenge

REJECTION
Addiction
Compulsions
Seeks acceptance
Unworthiness
Withdrawal

STUPOR & PRAYERLESSNESS
Distanced from God
"Cold" love
Distracted
Spiritual blindness
Laziness
Deceived self-appraisal

SEXUAL IMPURITY
Lust
Seductiveness
Masturbation
Fornication
Adultery
Frigidity
Homosexuality
Pornography

HEAVINESS
Depression
Despair
Self-pity
Loneliness
Unconfessed sin
Suicidal thoughts

PRIDE
Vain
Self-righteous
Self-centered
Insensitive
Materialistic
Seeks positions

REBELLION
Self-willed
Stubborn
Pouting
Strife
Factious
Divisive
Anger leads to argument
Independent
Unteachable

IDOLATRY
Frustrated
Hopeless
Greedy/selfish
Financial problems
Wrong goals/decisions
Living a lie
Apathetic

JEALOUSY
Spiteful
Gossip/slander
Betrayal
Critical nature
Judgmental
Suspicious

RELIGIOSITY
Seeks activities
No spiritual power
Spiritual blindness
Hypocritical

FEAR & INSECURITY
Inferiority
Inadequacy
Timidity
Pleasing people, not God
Lack of trust/worry
Phobias
Perfectionism
Dread of failure
Inability to set goals
"Motor-mouth"

Refer to the following pages on *Identifying Strongholds Through Their Symptoms* to determine which symptoms and strongholds are applicable to you. Before you continue, remind yourself that a stronghold is a "demonic fortress of influence" from which spirits function in the following ways.

- **Control, dictate, and influence your attitudes and behavior.**

- **Oppress and discourage you.**

- **Filter and color how you view or react to situations, circumstances, or people.**

As **you** desire to draw close to God, **He** will draw close to you. The words of Jeremiah are particularly applicable here: *"'For I know the plans I have for you,' declares the Lord, 'plans to prosper you and not to harm you, plans to give you hope and a future. Then you will call upon me and come and pray to me, and I will listen to you. You will seek me and find me when you seek me with all your heart. I will be found by you,' declares the Lord, 'and will bring you back from captivity' "* (Jeremiah 29:11-14).

| **Step One** | ## Identify Strongholds Through Their Symptoms |

Instructions

- Examine the following specific strongholds. Consider if the verses listed describe your situation or condition.

- Identify any of the accompanying symptoms that may be present in your life. Ponder the definitions. (The Holy Spirit may bring other meanings to mind too.)

- Use a scale of 1 to 10 beside each symptom. A stronghold is present when one or more of the symptoms has been habitually present in your life. (Your spouse, family members, or close friends may be helpful as you embark on this. Just ask them to refrain from accusation. Don't spend time denying what they suggest or trying to defend yourself!)

DECEIT

"If we claim to have fellowship with him yet walk in the darkness, we lie and do not live by the truth....If we claim to be without sin, we deceive ourselves and the truth is not in us" (1 John 1:6,8). *"The heart is deceitful above all things and beyond cure. Who can understand it?"* (Jeremiah 17:9). *"If anyone considers himself religious and yet does not keep a tight rein on his tongue, he deceives himself and his religion is worthless"* (James 1:26).

It is best to deal with this stronghold first. Satan's initial interaction with mankind involved deception. Since your soul (mind, will, and emotion) is the battleground, you need **to see clearly** the nature of those areas you have yielded to the enemy.

Symptom:	Definition:
☐ Lying	Falsifying information with desire to deceive
☐ Fantasies	Fanciful thoughts that have little credibility
☐ Delusions	Deceiving self into believing lies; often used to cover painful experiences from the past
☐ Rationalizations	Reasoning with desire to gloss over problems; attempting to deal with serious problem superficially; making excuses to justify behavior
☐ Wrong doctrine / misuse of Scripture	Reasoning a conclusion or position, then using the Bible to support the conclusion

BITTERNESS

"Do not let any unwholesome talk come out of your mouths, but only what is helpful for building others up according to their needs, that it may benefit those who listen. And do not grieve the Holy Spirit of God, with whom you were sealed for the day of redemption. Get rid of all bitterness, rage and anger, brawling and slander, along with every form of malice" (Ephesians 4:29-31). *"Therefore I will not keep silent; I will speak out in the anguish of my spirit, I will complain in the bitterness of my soul"* (Job 7:11).

The stronghold of bitterness may be present when you **habitually** feel one or more of the following symptoms when thinking of a particular person, place, or event. You may act kindly toward those who have no emotional involvement in your life but respond in defensive anger toward family or friends from whom you perceive an attack that isn't really there. Unforgiveness, in particular, puts you in a **prison of torment** (see Matthew 18:34,35) and brings pain to the one you have refused to forgive. According to Hebrews 12:15, a special problem with bitterness occurs: It **causes trouble** and **defiles the relationships** of others who are not even linked to the original painful event. For instance, unresolved bitterness toward parents often can show up later in a marriage and hinder bonding between the spouses.

Rejection had dominated Bob's life. Although popular and exuberant, his emotions were plagued by the memory of his mother's words: "When you were born, I cursed when I found out you weren't the girl baby I had so wanted." Subsequent illnesses and hospitalizations during his youth added to Bob's sense of being unwanted. He compensated through addictions to food and alcohol. He also sought acceptance through kind acts and abundant friendliness with everyone he encountered, hoping that they would genuinely like him. When Bob understood this rejection to be a stronghold, he renounced its effect on his life through the blood of Jesus, and sought the Spirit's infilling of assurance of God's love and acceptance. Overwhelming praise to God followed as he realized that the righteousness of Christ was his security and affirmation.

Symptom:	Definition:
☐ Resentment	Continuous begrudging attitude toward someone
☐ Hate	Intense aversion or animosity toward someone
☐ Unforgiveness	Inability to emotionally release someone
☐ Anger	Feelings of wrath or rage
☐ Violence	Emotional outrage enacting physical abuse
☐ Revenge	Desire for retaliation

HEAVINESS

"How long, O Lord? Will you forget me forever? How long will you hide your face from me? How long must I wrestle with my thoughts and every day have sorrow in my heart? How long will my enemy triumph over me? Look on me and answer, O Lord my God. Give light to my eyes or I will sleep in death" (Psalm 13:1-3). *"Among those nations you will find no repose, no resting place for the sole of your foot. There the Lord will give you an anxious mind, eyes weary with longing, and a despairing heart"* (Deuteronomy 28:65).

We know from Scripture that God desires you to have a childlike faith in Him that trusts wholeheartedly and absolutely in His love and mercies. The spirit of heaviness induces you to be convinced that your condition is **hopeless**: that no one cares, that even if circumstances improve, it's only temporary and you'll be miserable again; your life is a **cycle of sorrow** and you can't seem to get off the downward spiral.

Symptom:	Definition:
☐ Depression	Feelings of sorrow, despondency, dejection
☐ Despair	An overwhelming lack of hope
☐ Self-pity	A pattern of feeling sorry for yourself
☐ Loneliness	A sense of detachment or separation from others
☐ Unconfessed sin	Avoiding admission to God of known iniquity
☐ Suicidal thoughts	A strong desire to end your life

JEALOUSY

"Then the Lord said to Cain, 'Why are you angry? Why is your face downcast? If you do what is right, will you not be accepted? But if you do not do what is right, sin is crouching at your door; it desires to have you, but you must master it'" (Genesis 4:6-7). *"You are still worldly. For since there is jealousy and quarreling among you, are you not worldly?"* (1 Corinthians 3:3). *"Whenever one comes to see me, he speaks falsely, while his heart gathers slander; then he goes out and spreads it abroad"* (Psalm 41:6).

Like Cain, when you focus on the behavior and attitudes of others, you can develop a **judgmental posture** toward them. Rather than regarding them more highly than yourself as Scripture exhorts and respecting them for their godliness, you may begin to actively seek out their "warts"; you keep attuned to bad reports about that individual. By comparison, you appear better in your own mind.

Symptom:	Definition:
☐ Spiteful	Malicious attitude intending evil toward others
☐ Gossip/slander	Pattern of sharing detrimental information about someone with those not part of the problem or solution; telling part of the truth with a desire to hurt
☐ Betrayal	Breaking faith and turning against others
☐ Critical nature	Habitual pattern of fault-finding; never satisfied
☐ Judgmental	Feeling better about yourself by evaluating others in a way that predetermines their failure of some prescribed standard or criterion
☐ Suspicious	Pattern of distrusting and doubting the motives of others

CONFUSION / DOUBT and UNBELIEF

"If any of you lacks wisdom, he should ask God, who gives generously to all without finding fault, and it will be given to him. But when he asks, he must believe and not doubt, because he who doubts is like a wave of the sea, blown and tossed by the wind. That man should not think he will receive anything from the Lord; he is a double-minded man, unstable in all he does" (James 1:5-8). *"Jesus replied, 'No one who puts his hand to the plow and looks back is fit for service in the kingdom of God'"* (Luke 9:62). *"'Come,' he said. Then Peter got down out of the boat, and walked on the water and came to Jesus. But when he saw*

Kim discovered as she talked with her sister and her mother that rejection had been a characteristic of her family for four generations! In each generation, the women, controlled by the fear of rejection, gave themselves over to sexual promiscuity. This stronghold had manifested its presence in her by feelings of inadequacy and unworthiness. She appeared pleasant enough on the outside, but no one felt they really knew the "real" Kim. Believing that if people ever got close to her they wouldn't like what they found, she withdrew from intimacy. This carried over into a deep hurt in the relationship with her husband and son, who always felt that they were the cause of the emotional distance. When Kim renounced the generational stronghold of rejection and confessed to God the sins she had committed through its influence, she found forgiveness, freedom, and cleansing. As she became secure in her acceptance through the finished work of the cross, she was able to pray with boldness for God to use her as a vessel of blessing to others whether they "liked" her or not!

Jerry had grown up with a father who was a successful workaholic. Although he lacked for nothing material-ly, he never sensed much warmth or compassion from his parents. Then, when Jerry was still in his early teens, his father died very suddenly. His large family was left with little support, and insecurity and fear became the dominating fac-tors in the young man's life. Vowing to himself that he would never be poor again, Jerry worked hard at his business, making many ene-mies along the way because of his constant dissatisfac-tion with their performance as employees. A stronghold of idolatry brought reliance on the wealth he had accu-mulated rather than a prayerful dependency on God. Arguments over money dominated his marriage. Distrust and greed permeat-ed his home and business relationships. No one could "stand in his face" and tell him what to do. Finally, as his marriage disintegrated and his business gave signs of going under, Jerry renounced the strongholds of insecurity and fear

the wind, he was afraid and, beginning to sink, cried out, 'Lord, save me!' Immediately Jesus reached out his hand and caught him. 'You of little faith,'' he said, 'why did you doubt?' " (Matthew 14:29-31).

If you have entered into your relationship with Jesus based on a faulty under-standing of **Who He is**, you will be unable to grasp how high and wide and deep is His love for you. He is LORD, and as such desires **Lordship in your life.** If you are focusing more on the adverse circumstances in your life rather than on the One Who can free you, you are listening to the spirit of confusion. When you truly com-prehend the enormity of your sin and the vastness of His atonement on your behalf, you can then persevere in the "arena of suffering" that your earthly life calls for. Assured of His plan, you may be confident that His purpose and His presence will continue without fail.

Symptom:	Definition:
☐ Suspicious	Doubt or disbelief in God's promises
☐ Apprehensive	Anxiously fearful that God will not fulfill His plans for your good or that He "has it in for you"
☐ Indecisive	Intimate trust in Jesus is non-existent; double-minded anguish from indecision
☐ Skeptical	Continuous pattern of questioning and hesitancy to trust God
☐ Unsettled	Unable to experience *fruit of the Spirit* in your life

REJECTION

"He has alienated my brothers from me; my acquaintances are completely estranged from me. My kinsmen have gone away, my friends have forgotten me" (Job 19:13-14). *"Scorn has broken my heart and has left me helpless; I looked for sympathy, but there was none, for comforters, but I found none"* (Psalm 69:20).

When you feel that you **really don't matter** to others, the inner pain can be crippling. To avoid having to face the pain, this spirit induces you to compensate by just **coping:** You might avoid those whom you feel might bring you distress; you might escape through chemical means to ease the pain; you might act with-out care or concern about how your actions may affect others around you; or you might try to do acts of kindness in a desperate attempt to "earn" love and accep-tance.

Symptom:	Definition:
☐ Addiction	Obsession, intense preoccupation, or habit detrimental to important relationships
☐ Compulsions	Irrational obsession to act without forethought or regard to outcome
☐ Seek acceptance	Acting in kindness and friendliness with underlying motive to forestall rejection
☐ Unworthiness	Feeling unacceptable or inferior; never feeling like you can ever "measure up"
☐ Withdrawal	Removing self emotionally or physically from real or perceived hurtful and rejecting situations

PRIDE

"By your great skill in trading you have increased your wealth, and because of your wealth your heart has grown proud" (Ezekiel 28:5). *"I will break down your stubborn pride and make the sky above you like iron and the ground beneath you like bronze"* (Leviticus 26:19). *"There are those who curse their fathers and do not bless their mothers; those who are pure in their own eyes and yet are not cleansed of their filth; those whose eyes are ever so haughty, whose glances are so disdainful"* (Proverbs 30:11-13).

As a culture, Americans are obsessed with **image and appearance.** The focus on maintaining youthful health has surpassed stewardship of the body and has become an idol. We know more about fat grams than we do about the standards of holy living in Proverbs. The image we project through our homes, vehicles, attire, and activities becomes the means to our personal sense of worth. We not only have no desire to emulate the life standards of our parents, we pretty much have disassociated ourselves with them, either geographically or socially. Because God gives grace to the humble, the spirit of pride influences a person to focus instead on **self-gratification and personal fulfillment.** In our desire to appear "Christian," we feel better about what we **don't do** that's "evil" than about the "good" that God wants to do in and through us.

Symptom:	Definition:
☐ Vain	Conceited pretension about own importance
☐ Self-righteous	High opinion of own moral position compared to that of others

that had made money his idol and had shaped his disbelieving view of God's ability to meet his need. As the Holy Spirit brought conviction of the sins he had committed against so many people, he purposed to approach each one to seek forgiveness and make restitution wherever appropriate. His priorities shifted to God and family, then to close friends and business.

☐ Self-centered	Obsessive egocentric pattern of thinking; "the world revolves around me"	
☐ Insensitive	Unaware of impact on others; a bull-in-a-china-shop atmosphere created	
☐ Materialistic	Obsessive desire to acquire and hoard in order to gain recognition or prestige	
☐ Seeks positions	Viewing people and resources as means of fulfilling ego needs; relationships have no worth except to advance self	

RELIGIOSITY

"I know your deeds; you have a reputation of being alive, but you are dead. Wake up! Strengthen what remains and is about to die, for I have not found your deeds complete in the sight of my God. Remember, therefore, what you have received and heard; obey it, and repent" (Revelation 3:1-3). *"In the same way, on the outside you appear to people as righteous but on the inside you are full of hypocrisy and wickedness"* (Matthew 23:28).

Maybe you have been a believer for many years, serving the needs of the kingdom even to the point of burnout. People you have ministered to have been strengthened and encouraged, yet your own walk with Jesus has become impersonal and shallow. You may be at the point of going through the motions with no sense of loving God with all your heart, soul, and strength. Because others have always seen you as a spiritual pillar of strength, you feel you must **maintain that facade,** even if your inward pain is unbearable.

Symptom: **Definition:**

☐ Seeks activities	Intimate relationship with Jesus is non-existent; underlying attitude that "I must earn God's love; He will only love and accept me if I keep busy for Him"
☐ No spiritual power	Presence of the nature, character, or power of Jesus Christ lacking even after many years of religious practice
☐ Spiritual blindness	Unable to know the will of God or to receive guidance by His Spirit
☐ Hypocritical	Expressing truths and performing actions that may bless others but do not really emanate from your own life

As the oldest in a large family, Kerry had keenly felt the weight of responsibility, particularly after her father left. As a teenager, she had watched her mother struggle to raise the younger children. The devotion that her mother once had expressed toward God turned to bitterness. Kerry's outlook on life became imprisoned by fear — fear of abandonment, fear of poverty, fear that she was an inadequate wife and mother. Fear so consumed her that serious illnesses began to take their toll on her body. The myriad of prescription drugs she became dependent upon after her many surgeries left her depressed. She felt encompassed by a spirit of heaviness. As she saw these same fears springing up in her children, Kerry despaired. Then a trusted friend shared her own story of freedom from demonic influence, and Kerry began to hope. As they went over a list of possible strongholds, Kerry felt condemned because she saw herself in so many categories. Her friend reassured

INDEPENDENCE and DIVORCE

"The eye cannot say to the hand, 'I don't need you!' And the head cannot say to the feet, 'I don't need you!' (1 Corinthians 12:21). *"Plans fail for lack of counsel, but with many advisors they succeed"* (Proverbs 15:22). *"They went out from us, but they did not really belong to us. For if they had belonged to us, they would have remained with us; but their going showed that none of them belonged to us"* (1 John 2:19). *" 'For this reason a man will leave his father and mother and be united to his wife, and the two will become one flesh.' So they are no longer two, but one. Therefore what God has joined together, let man not separate"* (Matthew 19:5-6).

When you feel disconnected from others (family members, neighbors, co-workers, fellow believers, schoolmates), you tend to rely on your own efforts for decision. **"He who relies on himself for advice has a fool for a counselor"** says just what you really don't want to hear. While we may desperately wish that someone would make the effort to reach in past your abrasive or withdrawn demeanor, you aren't so sure that you want the responsibilities that come with relationship.

"Divorce" is not necessarily related to marriage. It can manifest itself in any interpersonal situations in which you walk away physically or emotionally due to real or perceived hurt. If you feel that **belonging to others is optional**, you then can justify why you can separate yourself from them. You are able to rationalize that it is easier (or more beneficial) for others if you simply leave rather than confront issues or sins that need to be addressed. Ultimately, the spirit of divorce leads to unforgiveness, bitterness, and guilt.

Symptom:	Definition:
☐ Insensitivity	Unaware of impact on others; a bull-in-a-china shop atmosphere created
☐ Loneliness	Sense of detachment or separation from others
☐ Self-determination	Relying solely on own analysis and appraisal for personal decisions
☐ Aloofness	Unresponsive to needs of others
☐ Withdrawal	Removing self emotionally or physically from real or perceived hurtful and rejecting situations
☐ Excuse making	Rationalizing with intent to blame other(s) for hurt or impasse in a relationship
☐ Lack of trust	Unable to rely/depend on others; underlying attitude, *"If you hurt me or let me down, I'm gone."* Places incredible pressure on relationship to never confront problems
☐ "Martyr complex"	Deceived sense that your leaving will actually *benefit* others, and that you won't be missed

her that God loved her and had given her the power of the Name of Jesus and His work on the cross to vanquish these spiritual menaces. As she prayed to renounce the strongholds of fear and heaviness, Kerry sensed a lightness she had forgotten. Joy lit her face as she praised God; her countenance glowed! As she sought God to fill her with the power of His Spirit, her tongue loosened and she boldly began sharing with her friends and family all that God had done for her.

Irritability and anger over minor provocations marked Karen's daily life. She had grown up as a pastor's daughter in a large and active household. Then her mother came down with a debilitating disease. Unable to cope, her father ran off with the church secretary, leaving the family destitute and forsaken. The children, teens at this point, managed to balance studies with care for their mother, but bitterness became the lens through which Karen viewed the world. She still attended church services, but God seemed remote and uncaring. A stronghold of prayerlessness characterized her walk with God; she served Him out of a sense of obligation rather than from a love relationship. One day while visiting us, she became blinded by using the wrong contact lens solution. For three days she sat in her darkness, crying out to God. Through the Holy Spirit she recognized the prison her bitterness had kept her in:

STUPOR / PRAYERLESSNESS

"As it is written, 'God gave them a spirit of stupor, eyes so that they could not see and ears so that they could not hear, to this very day'" (Romans 11:8). "For day after day they seek me out; they seem eager to know my ways, as if they were a nation that does what is right and has not forsaken the commands of its God. They ask me for just decisions and seem eager for God to come near them" (Isaiah 58:2). "And do this, understanding the present time. The hour has come for you to wake up from your slumber, because our salvation is nearer now than when we first believed" (Romans 13:11).

Because you feel as though the Holy Spirit has not been revealing anything to your spirit, your expectations of Divine involvement and intervention are almost nil. You may have become so **wrapped up** in the cares and activities of life that you don't spend much time seeking the Lord. You **fail to appreciate** the "little" blessings and kindnesses that God has been pouring out. Perhaps you are so desperate for one key answer to prayer that you have disregarded His other activities all around you. You fail to see that God might be allowing various trials in your life to conform your character to Christ's; you would rather remain in the "comfort zone" as far as opportunities for deepening your faith are concerned.

Symptom:	Definition:
☐ Distanced from God	God viewed as "unconcerned"; sense of hopelessness felt when presenting needs to Him; underlying thought of "If I pray, He won't answer."
☐ "Cold" love	Prayer viewed as obligation of religious practice rather than communication with Someone loved
☐ Distracted	Unable to focus on communication with God; thoughts and worries invade prayer
☐ Spiritual blindness	Unable to know God's will or receive guidance by His Spirit
☐ Laziness	Resistant to industrious pursuit of God's plans for your life; "your walk doesn't match your talk"
☐ Deceived self-appraisal	Unable to detect personal sin that may be hindering your prayers

REBELLION

"There is no fear of God before his eyes. For in his own eyes he flatters himself too much to detect or hate his sin. The words of his mouth are wicked and deceitful; he has ceased to be wise and to do good" (Psalm 36:1-3). *"But my people would not listen to me; Israel would not submit to me. So I gave them over to their stubborn hearts to follow their own devices"* (Psalm 81:11,12).

Rebellion festers privately in the heart of the person who is open to it but ultimately shows its hand in a public way. Some strongholds remain hidden from interference in the lives of others, but the spirit of rebellion searches for others with whom to stir up dissension. The weapon wielded by this spirit is **the tongue** — *"a fire, a world of evil among the parts of the body"* (James 3:6). Rather than listening to others, a person influenced by a rebellious spirit pushes for his or her own way vocally and forcefully, unconcerned for the wounded relationships left in the wake.

Symptom:	Definition:
☐ Self-willed	Concerned with wanting own way more than the will of God or others in authority
☐ Stubborn	Obstinate attitude toward others and reluctance to accept truth or help from others
☐ Pouting	Visible sulking behavior, indicating rejection of a truth or situation
☐ Strife	Clashing; creating unnecessary conflict in relationships
☐ Factious	Joining together with other dissenting people with desire to conspire or plot
☐ Divisive	Encouraging disagreement rather than seeking points of agreement; often playing "devil's advocate"
☐ Anger leads to argument	Hostile feelings leading to arguments often disguised as desire to explain your position or build your case
☐ Independent	Maintaining self-reliant and separate position from others; unable to belong
☐ Unteachable	Continuing to return to same errant position; often mocking those trying to help

consumed by unforgiveness for her father, resentment toward her mother, and anger at God for allowing it all to happen. Karen renounced the spirit of bitterness and claimed the power of Christ's atonement and acceptance of her as His own. She prayed for the work of God in her own heart to forgive and to believe in God's power to bring good out of all this. That afternoon, her vision cleared. She sat down and wrote a letter to her father asking forgiveness for her bitterness against him all this time. He responded immediately, beseeching her to come see him. A great healing had begun.

FEAR and INSECURITY

Division was in the air at First Church. Behind the facade of full pews each Sunday morning was intense grumbling and murmuring among the parishioners. Rumors of sinful conduct by the pastor had surfaced. When the issues were brought before the pastor by several members of leadership, he admitted that some of the allegations might appear true but that he didn't regard them as serious. He felt that he was doing a good job as senior pastor and that the pressures and stresses he faced on behalf of the flock were causing these "problems." He never viewed them as sins requiring repentance. As word got out, a group of the congregation responded with outrage and self-righteous pride. Rather than fasting and praying for the pastor to repent or approaching the elders to take further steps, this disgruntled group left in protest. The ones that remained looked down on the departees and for awhile felt the body was better off without them. But as the sermons became more watered-down and the pastor's attitude grew increasingly standoffish, division brewed again. A second

"Fear and trembling have beset me; horror has overwhelmed me. I said, 'Oh, that I had the wings of a dove! I would fly away and be at rest — I would flee far away and stay in the desert'" (Psalm 55:5-7). *"Strengthen the feeble hands, steady the knees that give way; say to those with fearful hearts, 'Be strong, do not fear'"* (Isaiah 35:3,4). *"What I feared has come upon me; what I dreaded has happened to me. I have no peace, no quietness; I have no rest, but only turmoil"* (Job 3:25,26).

Do you wonder why you often think, **"If I don't do it, it won't get done right?"** Maybe you are wrestling with what one writer has termed *False Expectations Appearing Real*. Perhaps you have projected your expectations of outcome onto others, causing them to feel anxious and pressured. You may be struggling with the heavy burden of responsibility to meet your perception of what constitutes "acceptable." The **task** seems much more important to you than the people you are with. If probed, you would be hard-pressed to come up with a reason why you are compelled **to do** rather than **to be.**

There are times when anyone would much rather be somewhere else than in the middle of the situation that is producing sweats and heart palpitations. However, the spirit of fear **consistently convinces you** that you have nothing worthwhile to contribute, that if you speak up no one will accept what you have to offer, and that people will just turn away from you. In effect, the hunger to **please those around you** surpasses your desire to obey what you know God wants you to do or say.

Symptom:	Definition:
☐ Inferiority	Feeling subordinate or lower than others
☐ Inadequacy	Feeling incompetent or inept in accomplishing things
☐ Timidity	Feelings of shyness, bashfulness, or cowardice; often leads to withdrawal from others
☐ Pleasing people, not God	Overly concerned about what others might think
☐ Lack of trust/ worry	Never feeling comfortable, lacking a sense of "belonging" to others; may *appear* friendly but have few or no deep friendships
☐ Phobias	Obsessive fear, aversion to, or dislike of a particular person or situation, often with no apparent foundation
☐ Perfectionist	Obsessive desire for flawlessness; inability to find satisfaction with self or others

☐ Dread of failure — Shame-based motivation with abnormal pressure to always succeed; you rely on self in times of pressure and fail to turn to or trust others

☐ Inability to set goals — Prolonged pattern of indecisiveness; feel threatened by potential confrontation in decision making process

☐ "Motor-mouth" — Constant chatter that precludes input from others

CONTROL

"For he says, 'By the strength of my hand I have done this, and by my wisdom, because I have understanding'" (Isaiah 10:13). "For by the grace given me I say to every one of you: Do not think of yourself more highly than you ought, but rather think of yourself with sober judgment, in accordance with the measure of faith God has given you" (Romans 12:3).

You feel that **your** input and decisions are key. In fact, you really don't trust that anyone else can see the whole picture as clearly as you can. You are willing to shoulder the responsibility but recognize the need for assistance, particularly if the participants are willing to **follow your suggestions**. If others offer advice, you tend to doubt both their capability and their motives; you are **driven even harder** to achieve the desired goal.

Symptom:	Definition:
☐ Manipulative	Desire to maneuver or orchestrate the lives of others for personal advantage
☐ Striving	Endeavoring and struggling to accomplish; difficult for you to just "be"
☐ Lacking trust	Inability to rely on others or to have confidence in God
☐ Worried	Continuous pattern of uneasiness and apprehension
☐ Insensitive	Unaware of impact on others; a bull-in-a-china-shop atmosphere created around self
☐ Desiring recognition	Seeking acclaim or notice for what you do
☐ Violent	Emotional outrage enacting physical abuse

wave of murmuring people approached the leadership and felt compelled to leave the church. (Three waves of departees occurred in less than two years.) The elders refused to confront the pastor with his ongoing sin. No one in any of the three waves seemed able to go on in their Christian walk. After two years we met with all three waves over a period of several days. It was then that they saw the stronghold of pride that was controlling not only the church they had fled but also themselves personally. As they all prayed to renounce the influence of the stronghold, compassion and mercy began to surface in their hearts. (A thought to ponder: As we were finishing our last meeting with the people, we commented that the situation in their church was similar to that of another church we had worked with several years earlier. As we named the town and state of that church, they named the church where the pastor prior to this one had gone in that same town. It was the same church — same pastor — and same stronghold among that flock!)

"Ron, I've been praying for you, and I think you have a stronghold of rebellion," I said. "I know that!" Ron shouted into the phone. "Why don't you call your mom," I suggested, "and ask her what symptoms of rebellion she sees in you." Ron pondered that idea, then phoned his mother, who lived out-of-state. Although he had maintained regular telephone contact with her, he had always felt uneasiness in her presence. "Mom, Mike thinks I have a stronghold of rebellion. Do you see this in me?" "Of course I do," she replied. "Our whole family has it!" As she scored Ron from 1 to 10 in intensity of symptoms, a picture emerged: strong will, stubbornness, independent spirit. Ron scored fairly low on strife and divisions and unteachableness. He called his brother and received scores almost identical to his mother's. Next came the real challenge: his ex-wife. She and Ron had maintained a friendly relationship during their years apart, and he knew he could trust her to be candid. Her first scores were similar to his family's evaluations, but then she surprised him with high scores on strife and anger that leads to arguments. "Why?" he asked. "My family gave me low

SEXUAL IMPURITY

"[The Gentiles] are darkened in their understanding and separated from the life of God because of the ignorance that is in them due to the hardening of their hearts. Having lost all sensitivity, they have given themselves over to sensuality so as to indulge in every kind of impurity, with a continual lust for more" (Ephesians 4:18,19). *"Let us behave decently, as in the daytime, not in orgies and drunkenness, not in sexual immorality and debauchery, not in dissension and jealousy"* (Romans 13:13).

Often sexual sin is done in the dark — figuratively and literally. A darkened understanding of God's standards of purity greatly decreases your sensitivity to the ever-increasing violations of those standards. The individual influenced by this spirit **throws off restraints** — first in the mind and then in the flesh. **Gratification** becomes the issue; the relationship becomes secondary. Even in regard to frigidity, the relationship has ceased to be the priority.

Symptom:	Definition:
☐ Lust	Lecherous desire to sexually possess someone forbidden by God's law
☐ Seductiveness	Using sexual arousal to allure interest
☐ Masturbation	Personal gratification as opposed to self-control
☐ Fornication	Sexual relationships between unmarried people
☐ Adultery	Sexual desire and/or relationships by married person outside of marriage
☐ Frigidity	Inhibited, indifferent, passionless view toward sexual relations
☐ Homosexuality	Sexual relationship with member of same gender
☐ Pornography	Desire for vicarious sexual arousal

IDOLATRY

"People who want to get rich fall into temptation and a trap and into many foolish and harmful desires that plunge men into ruin and destruction. For the love of money is a root of all kinds of evil. Some people, eager for money, have wandered from the faith and pierced themselves with many griefs" (1 Timothy 6:9-10).

A rich man was once asked, "How much money is enough?" He replied, "A little bit more." To crave and yearn for more of earth's treasures and pleasures defies God's will to "seek first the kingdom." You are **unable to be grateful** for what you have because you are disconnected from the Source of peace. "Happiness" seems to be just out of grasp. You long with all your heart for whatever you think will bring contentment. That becomes your next idol.

Symptom:	Definition:
☐ Frustrated	Continuous feelings of perplexity; nothing seems to go right
☐ Hopeless	Strong feelings of desperation and despondency
☐ Greedy/selfish	Stinginess or excessive self-indulgence
☐ Financial problems	Habitual pattern of bad financial decisions
☐ Wrong goals/ decisions	Outcome focused on temporal pleasures and material possessions
☐ Living a lie	Fear that others will discover the hollowness and superficiality of your life
☐ Apathetic	Unconcerned for the feelings or welfare of others

scores on those." She chuckled wryly, "They weren't married to you." Then she asked if there was a category for pouting. During their marriage he had reacted to disagreements with silent frowns and distancing — behaviors that had carried into other relationships as well. Ron set the phone down and prayed, renouncing in the strong name of Jesus the stronghold of rebellion that had plagued him since childhood. A new desire to fully yield to God and to serve others flooded him. He immediately made arrangements to move in with his widowed mother, and he was able over the course of two months to bring healing and freedom from her stronghold of rebellion through the power of the Holy Spirit.

Step Two | **Renounce the Strongholds**

Many have found it helpful to have a witness with them as they renounce the influence of the strongholds. A witness is beneficial not because you need others to help you demolish the strongholds, but **to remind and encourage you** later when Satan tries to convince you that nothing has changed. If you are married it is appropriate to have your spouse join you in praying through the strongholds that affect you, your marriage, and family. If you are not married or if your spouse is unwilling to help you renounce the stronghold's influence at this time, if possible, find someone close to you with whom to pray.

Each believer has the power of the Holy Spirit to renounce these strongholds with the authority of the name of Jesus our Lord. We *"have divine power to demolish strongholds"* (2 Corinthians 10:4). After you have recognized the symptoms that identify the stronghold, renounce the stronghold and confess any sins that you have committed that relate to its influence. **Pray, using the authority of the Name of the Lord Jesus** and the **power of His shed blood to demolish these strongholds and renounce their influence in your life.** Consider the power and authority that Jesus has given His followers as revealed in the following verses.

- *"He appointed twelve — designating them apostles — that they might be with him and that he might send them out to preach and to have **authority to drive out demons**"* (Mark 3:14,15, emphasis added).

- *"They went out and preached that people should repent. They **drove out many demons** and anointed many sick people with oil and healed them"* (Mark 6:12,13, emphasis added).

- *"And these signs will accompany those who believe: **In my name they will drive out demons**"* (Mark 16:17, emphasis added).

- *"The seventy-two returned with joy and said, '**Lord, even the demons submit to us in your name.**'..'I have given you **authority to trample** on snakes and scorpions and **to overcome** all the power of the enemy; nothing will harm you"* (Luke 10:17,19, emphasis added).

Remember that many strongholds hide behind a **veneer of deception**. As we quoted Frangipane earlier, "Once a person is **deceived**, he does not **recognize** that he is deceived, **because he has been deceived.**" Lying, fantasies, delusions, rationalizations, wrong doctrine, and misuse of Scripture will hinder your arrival at the truth concerning the strongholds that influence and oppress you. We recommend that you **first renounce the stronghold of deceit.**

After you have exercised the authority of the name of Jesus to demolish the strongholds, Satan will try to convince you that nothing has happened. But God's Word is true. **We have overcome Satan by the blood of the Lamb and by the word of our testimony!** Proclaim the victory of the Cross!

BEFORE YOU PRAY, read Chapter 5, *Taking Back Surrendered Ground,* to determine which **countervailing spiritual truths** God has for you.

If you are unsure how to pray, you might consider something like this:

Father in heaven, I recognize the power You have given me by the shed blood of Jesus to demolish strongholds in my life. I confess that I have given a foothold to the sin(s) of _____ . I renounce the stronghold of _____ by the authority of the Name of Jesus Christ according to Your Word. I take back through Your power that ground that I surrendered to the enemy and pray that You will fill me with _____ by Your Holy Spirit so that this area of my life will be in conformity to the image of Christ. In Jesus' Name I pray. Amen.

After demolishing the strongholds, remember four important things.

1. Renounce Satanic Thoughts
• Begin to *take captive every thought to make it obedient to Christ* (see 2 Corinthians 10:5). Do not let the cycle of thoughts, emotions, actions, habits, and strongholds begin again. As you are being harassed, especially by condemning or critical thoughts, **renounce those thoughts** in the name of the Lord Jesus. Don't give Satan a foothold by entertaining demonic spirits.

2. Put On Your Spiritual Armor
• **Take back the surrendered ground** where strongholds once influenced your life. Choose to put on the **spiritual armor** that God has given: the **belt of truth** — trust in the Lord Jesus, Who declared Himself to be the Truth; the **breastplate of righteousness** — assurance that the blood of Christ enables us to stand righteous before the Father; feet fitted with **readiness from the gospel of peace** — prepared for His service because **He** is sanctifying us through and through; the **shield of faith** — which by God's power extinguishes the enemy's darts; the **helmet of salvation** — which focuses our minds on God and guards against further enemy intrusion; the **sword of the Spirit** — which we wield as we immerse ourselves in His Word; and **prayer in the Spirit** — that we may be alert and available at all times for communion with God.

3. Enlist the Help of Others

• **Seek help** from your spouse, family, or other believers with whom you have a close relationship. God will use them to help you discern the means He has provided for you to **meet the seven needs** He created in us. Otherwise, you may seek a carnal way to meet these needs and provide a foothold for the strongholds to return.

4. Review the Stronghold List Periodically

• Go back over the list of strongholds and the accompanying symptoms to see if any **patterns** are returning. This last recommendation has been one of the hardest for people to do. Often they will tell us that they have a fear of looking at the stronghold sheet again because of what they might find. But God isn't exposing these strongholds to condemn you. He is seeking you out so that you will **confess your sins**. Through His forgiveness and cleansing, your **fellowship with Him** might once again be restored (see 1 John 1:9).

Do not be afraid to go back and *Demolish Strongholds* whenever anything is blocking the Truth and Love of Jesus in your life.

Chapter 5

Taking Back Surrendered Ground

Jesus Christ is the personification of God's character, e.g., His wisdom, understanding, counsel. Jesus desires His people to **experience Him** completely, not just His love, His truth, and the fruit of that love and truth in your life. He also desires for you to **appropriate His character.** When you live under the influence of strongholds, they block the visible evidences of Christ in you. When the strongholds have been demolished, you can **pray in agreement** with the Holy Spirit for God to produce His spiritual truths in you. Through His grace, reclaim the previously surrendered ground of your soul.

> *"The Spirit of the Lord will rest on him —
> the Spirit of wisdom and of understanding,
> the Spirit of counsel and of power,
> the Spirit of knowledge and of the fear of the Lord"*
>
> (Isaiah 11:2).

REMEMBER: The following diagram illustrates the effect that the spirits dwelling in their strongholds have on certain areas of your mind, will, and emotions. Again, those areas of your life that you surrender to sin are the fertile ground for demonic spirits to influence your thoughts, feelings, and decisions. As your thoughts are distorted by those spirits, they are able to construct a fortress around that area of your soul. The truths of God do not penetrate the barrier that your sinful choices have allowed to stand.

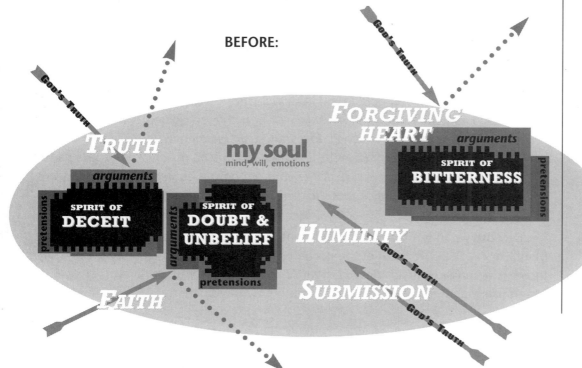

BEFORE:

Mara could not believe that God would abandon her at her most desperate hour. For the whole fourteen years of her troubled marriage, hadn't she tried to be the perfect wife and mother? During her unhappy childhood Mara had vowed that she would never be like her own mother, who had browbeaten her husband and made Mara feel inadequate and worthless. Mara couldn't see that the more she focused on not being bitter like her mother, the more the bitterness in her manifested itself toward anyone who didn't meet her expectations. Unfortunately, her very busy husband most often fit that category. For years Mara had pursued a frantic search for peace and joy, overspending their budget and discarding hobbies and jobs repeatedly. The growing despair and captivity caused by her bitterness blinded her to the caring believers God continued to send her way. She could only view them with

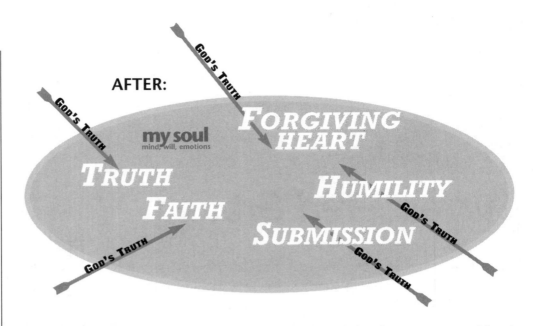

After the influence of the spirits in the strongholds has been renounced by the power and authority of the Lord Jesus Christ, you are able to discern the truths that God wants to reveal to you. The strongholds that were in your soul are replaced by the truth and love that He has wanted to fill you with all along!

Instructions

Meditate on the following verses, putting your name into the verse to **personalize** the truths in it. Pray for sensitivity to the Holy Spirit's promptings as He reveals ways in which to **apply** the spiritual truth He wishes to develop in you. Some have found it helpful to use the paragraph beneath the verses as a prayer guide.

Stronghold   **Spiritual Truth**

DECEIT . . . . SPIRIT OF TRUTH

"Jesus said, 'If you hold to my teaching, you are really my disciples. Then you will know the truth, and the truth will set you free'" (John 8:31,32). *"Whoever would love life and see good days must keep his tongue from evil and his lips from deceitful speech. He must turn from evil and do good; he must seek peace and pursue it. For the eyes of the Lord are on the righteous and his ears are attentive to their prayer, but the face of the Lord is against those who do evil"* (1 Peter 3:10-12).

Because Satan is a liar and the father of lies, he has at his disposal many means of infiltrating the pure truth of the gospel. Paul warned Timothy to **stay away** from those who engage in godless chatter or quarreling about controversial topics. Recognize that some elements of falsehood may have penetrated your mind, will, and emotions. Renounce the work of Satan in those areas of your life and claim the victory of the blood of Christ as one of His redeemed. Heed Paul's admonition to Timothy, appropriating its truths by the Spirit: *"Flee the evil desires of youth, and pursue righteousness, faith, love and peace, along with those who call on the Lord out of a pure heart"* (2 Timothy 2:22). Choose companions whose hearts are also set on loving obedience to God.

Stronghold	Spiritual Truth

BITTERNESS . . . . *FORGIVING HEART*

> *"If you forgive men when they sin against you, your heavenly Father will also forgive you. But if you do not forgive men their sins, your Father will not forgive your sins"* (Matthew 6:14,15). *"[Love] keeps no record of wrongs"* (1 Corinthians 13:5).

Ask God to fill you with the sacrificial love that He demonstrated by sending His Son to lay down His life for you. **Pray for those who have mistreated you**, remembering that the only One Who can handle vengeance without sinning is God. If you are to walk in the steps of Jesus (see 1 Peter 2:21), if you want to call your Heavenly Father *"Abba"* (see Romans 8:15-17), you must learn to **suffer as He did.** This will mean that the hurt you receive from those close to you must be seen from God's vantage point. He caused His own Son to suffer so that He would learn obedience (see Hebrews 5:8). As a wise friend once told us, "You will never learn to walk in the fullness of Jesus until you can wash the feet of Judas."

Stronghold	Spiritual Truth

HEAVINESS . . . . *PRAISE*

> *"To bestow on them a crown of beauty instead of ashes, the oil of gladness instead of mourning, and a garment of praise instead of a spirit of despair"* (Isaiah 61:3). *"Praise the Lord, O my soul, and forget not all his benefits, who forgives all your sins and heals all your diseases; who redeems your life from the pit and crowns you with love and compassion"* (Psalm 103:2-4).

Take back that ground where the enemy has sown depression, loneliness, self-pity — the "ashes" of hopelessness — and pray for God to plant in you a heart **willing to rejoice** in Him. As you express songs of praise to God for Who He is, He will deliver you from all your fears: *"I will extol the Lord at all times; his praise will always be on my lips. My soul will boast in the Lord; let the afflicted hear and rejoice. Glorify the Lord with me; let us exalt his name together. I sought the Lord and he answered me; he delivered me from all my fears"* (Psalm 34:1-4). You will receive comfort and strength from the One Who has promised to **be with you always**.

suspicion and distrust. Countless sessions of professional counseling had left her convinced that she was a perpetual victim, powerless and persecuted. Isolating herself from anyone who might help her, Mara challenged God to supernaturally change her husband and marriage. Refusing to appropriate God's grace and humbly ask her parents' forgiveness for her years of bitterness toward them, hopelessness and heaviness engulfed her. Mara was herself a prisoner of that demonic spirit.

"I've been one lucky guy," Cal thought. Ever since he could remember, he'd wanted to fly. Now he was an airline pilot with a beautiful wife, comfortable home, smart kids. He was recognized in his community as a man of high moral fiber, active in influential civic groups. So what were these divorce papers he was holding in his shaking hand? What had happened to his orderly, orchestrated little world? Sure, over the years Sara had dragged him to various counseling sessions, hoping that somehow they could develop warm and meaningful communication in their strained relationship, but what did those counselors know, he thought. Anger and frustration burned in him. He reluctantly called a friend, who listened sympathetically and then recommended that he call us. Cal was a charming, likable guy, but he expected life to operate from his point of view. As Mike probed around a little, we discovered a man who had made it on his own, a man almost oblivious to the needs of others. Sue walked into the room as we were talking, and Mike asked Cal to repeat a point he had been making about his wife. Sue countered, "I don't think any woman would respond positively to what you just said." Cal had never paid much attention to female perspectives, and he fired question after question at Sue, who unveiled to him a totally new approach to his wife. He was astonished, yet

Stronghold	Spiritual Truth
JEALOUSY	*SACRIFICIAL LOVE*

"But since we belong to the day, let us be self-controlled, putting on faith and love as a breastplate, and the hope of salvation as a helmet. Therefore encourage one another and build each other up" (1 Thessalonians 5:8,11). *"Love is patient, love is kind. It does not envy, it does not boast, it is not proud. It is not rude, it is not self-seeking, it is not easily angered, it keeps no record of wrongs. Love does not delight in evil but rejoices with the truth. It always protects, always trusts, always hopes, always perseveres"* (1 Corinthians 13:4-7).

Sacrificial love seeks to benefit others even at a **cost to yourself:** *"Do nothing out of selfish ambition or vain conceit, but in humility consider others better than yourselves"* (Philippians 2:3). You must choose to turn away from gossip, slander, and godless chatter in order to build one another up. Be sure to examine your inner motives in all you say and do, and ask yourself, **"Would Jesus say or do this?"** Jealousy causes you to delight when a perceived competitor stumbles so that you might then look better. Therefore, God would desire for you to have *"a pure heart and a good conscience and a sincere faith"* (1 Timothy 1:5) — the qualities of Christ that you need in your soul to take back the surrendered ground of jealousy and distrust.

Stronghold	Spiritual Truth
CONFUSION	*FAITH*
(DOUBT AND UNBELIEF)	

"Do you not know? Have you not heard? The Lord is the everlasting God, the Creator of the ends of the earth. He will not grow tired or weary, and his understanding no one can fathom. He gives strength to the weary and increases the power of the weak" (Isaiah 40:28,29). *"To those who through the righteousness of our God and Savior Jesus Christ have received a faith as precious as ours: Grace and peace be yours in abundance through the knowledge of God and of Jesus our Lord. His divine power has given us everything we need for life and godliness through our knowledge of him who called us by his own glory and goodness"* (2 Peter 1:2,3).

Meditate on the above verses, focusing on the **righteousness of Christ** and **His divine power.** God Who is your Creator knows your every fiber. He understands when you are weary and weak. He is the One Who sustains you when you feel lost and downcast. Reclaim that ground the enemy built upon by praying for *"the spirit of wisdom and revelation, so that you may know him better"* (Ephesians 1:17). Earnestly **seek Him** in the Word and be encouraged by the lives He continues to change around you. **Meditate** on the faith of your spiritual fore-fathers in Hebrews 11. **Pray** often throughout the day for His will to fulfill that **life and godliness** He has given you.

Stronghold	Spiritual Truth
REJECTION	*ACCEPTANCE*

"Praise be to the God and Father of our Lord Jesus Christ! In his great mercy he has given us new birth into a living hope through the resurrection of Jesus Christ from the dead, and into an inheritance that can never perish, spoil or fade — kept in heaven for you, who through faith are shielded by God's power until the coming of the salvation that is ready to be revealed in the last time" (1 Peter 1:3-5). *"But you are a chosen people, a royal priesthood, a holy nation, a people belonging to God, that you may declare the praises of him who called you out of darkness into his wonderful light"* (1 Peter 2:9).

How could you be any more acceptable to God, Who has declared you to be **His own treasure,** empowered by His Spirit to declare His praise! Praise God for this irrevocable truth. You have great purpose and meaning to God. His commands to His people Israel apply to you as well: *"To love the Lord your God, to walk in all his ways, to obey his commands, to hold fast to him and to serve him with all your heart and all your soul"* (Joshua 22:5). Pray for Him to reveal the **specific means** for you to enact these commands, step by step, and to fill you with joy as you realize how precious you are to Him. You have been purchased by His Son's blood and are His very own!

Stronghold	Spiritual Truth
PRIDE	*HUMILITY*

"Clothe yourselves with humility toward one another, because, 'God opposes the proud but gives grace to the humble.' Humble yourselves, therefore, under God's mighty hand, that he may lift you up in due time" (1 Peter 5:5-6). *"Be completely humble and gentle; be patient, bearing with one another in love"* (Ephesians 4:2). *"This is the one I esteem: he who is humble and contrite in spirit, and trembles at my word"* (Isaiah 66:2).

Always remember to thank God for the grace that He has promised to you as you **humble yourself** before His Lordship! See yourself as a **servant to others,** as though you were serving Christ Himself. Be sure that your heart attitude is **pure**. If ulterior motives for personal gain or recognition are there, repent and appropriate God's forgiveness and cleansing (see 1 John 1:9). Pray that God will provide **opportunities for spiritual fruit** — love, joy, peace, patience, kindness, goodness, faithfulness, gentleness, self-control — to be manifested as you put others ahead of yourself.

intrigued. Since his awkward flight schedule could be hindering his marriage, we confronted Cal with a proposition: Call both his father and father-in-law for discernment and ask them if his flying was contributing to his wife's unhappiness. Cal sank low in his chair. He truly loved his wife, but flying had been his passion. To his immense relief, both men reassured him that his problem lay not with his flight schedule but with the multitude of other activities he was immersed in when he was home. Sara and the children had felt neglected and unimportant to him. Cal began to see how his self-centered insensitivity to his wife had dammed up any hope in her for their marriage. When he repented of his self-righteous attitudes and hurtful disregard of his family, Cal was able to renounce the strongholds of pride and rebellion that had so closed his spirit to the promptings of God's Spirit. Cal then began a process of wooing back his wife, exposing to her a humble vulnerability that she had never before seen in him. He marveled at the depth of his wife's comments and conversation; he had previously never taken the time to explore her unique capabilities. Even the children rejoiced in the change in their dad. A new gentleness and warmth permeated their home. Cal and Sara were prepared to help other troubled couples in their church.

"What a pleasant neighborhood," Sue remarked as we drove to our dinner engagement. We took in the tidy lawns, modest but neat homes, and paraphernalia of youth: bikes, basketball hoops, swings. We had been invited by Jim and Gina, whom we had met briefly before. As soon as we entered their sunny home, Gina began a litany of apologies: "I'm so embarrassed to have people in. All our friends have such beautiful homes decorated by professionals, and this place needs so much work." Actually, we thought it was very comfortable, and we were surprised by her discomfort. As our relationship with Jim and Gina continued, we noted that envy and coveting had become almost an obsession for Gina. How others dressed, where they shopped, even what kind of car they drove meant a great deal to her. Her frustration at being a "have-not" was straining her relationship with her husband. His business had been slipping financially, and rather than emotionally supporting him during this trying time, Gina was nagging him for more funds. Soon all their conversations as a couple deteriorated into squabbles over money. Sue could see the tension in Gina, and gently asked to

Stronghold	Spiritual Truth
RELIGIOSITY	*PRAISE AND PEACE*

"'Love the Lord your God with all your heart and with all your soul and with all your strength and with all your mind' and, 'Love your neighbor as yourself.' 'You have answered correctly,' Jesus replied. 'Do this and you will live'" (Luke 10:27,28). "This is what the Sovereign Lord, the Holy One of Israel, says: 'In repentance and rest is your salvation, in quietness and trust is your strength, but you would have none of it'"* (Isaiah 30:15).

Set aside for yourself a **sabbatical** from church-related activities. Spend time quietly before God; ask Him to reveal to you different facets of Who He is. Ponder in the Word the different **names of God** and their implications for your life, e.g., the Prince of Peace, the Alpha and the Omega, etc. Allow the Spirit to well up within you a heart of praise for God. Ask Him to open your eyes to opportunities to serve Him by serving others **as He reveals them.** Resist attempts by well-meaning friends to get you back into the "old groove" unless God makes it clear that He is the one opening each door. **Be accountable** to your spouse or intimate circle of friends to move at the impulse of His love and not out of guilt or performance motivation.

Stronghold	Spiritual Truth
INDEPENDENCE **and DIVORCE**	*UNITY AND COMMITMENT*

"May the God who gives endurance and encouragement give you a spirit of unity among yourselves as you follow Christ Jesus, so that with one heart and mouth you may glorify the God and Father of our Lord Jesus Christ. Accept one another, then, just as Christ accepted you, in order to bring praise to God." (Romans 15:5-7). *"Just as each of us has one body with many members, and these members do not all have the same function, so in Christ we who are many form one body, and each member belongs to all the others"* (Romans 12:4,5).

Followers of Christ are each baptized by the Spirit into one body (see 1Corinthians 12:13). Proclaim this truth to your inner being: God has combined the members of the body so that there should be no division but that the parts should have **equal concern for each other.** With the spiritual gifts God has given to His body, you are to bring glory to Him by serving one another and the world. Will the world come to Christ if they do not see how Christians love and are committed to one another? Whether in a marriage, a family, a faith community or the workplace, pray for the will and the desire to **join with God** in the purpose He has for your life in conjunction with others. Ask for "spiritual eyes and ears" to recognize and understand your part in the Kingdom of God. Pray for the Spirit to pour into you a desire and understanding to be *"joined and held together by every supporting* *ligament*" in a faith body that is **growing and building itself up** in love as each part does its work (see Ephesians 4:16).

Stronghold	Spiritual Truth
STUPOR AND	.*PERSEVERANCE AND HOPE*
PRAYERLESSNESS	

"Therefore, since we have a great high priest who has gone through the heavens, Jesus the Son of God, let us hold firmly to the faith we profess. For we do not have a high priest who is unable to sympathize with our weaknesses, but we have one who has been tempted in every way, just as we are — yet was without sin. Let us then approach the throne of grace with confidence, so that we may receive mercy and find grace to help us in our time of need" (Hebrews 4:14-16). *"And we rejoice in the hope of the glory of God. Not only so, but we also rejoice in our sufferings, because we know that suffering produces perseverance; perseverance, character; and character, hope. And hope does not disappoint us, because God has poured out his love into our hearts by the Holy Spirit, whom he has given us"* (Romans 5:2-5).

Satan will often use two tactics to keep you from drawing near to God through prayer: (1) He may cause you to misperceive God's work of developing hope in you. God's plan is to use **suffering** to produce perseverance, character, and finally **hope** in you. As you suffer, Satan may convince you that your suffering is a sign of God's rejection. A coldness and distance toward God may enter your relationship with Him. (2) Even after you have confessed your sins and they are forgiven, Satan may use **"false guilt"** to keep you from approaching God. He will remind you of what you have done and also attempt to convince you that you must earn back God's love. The truth of the matter is that the sacrificial shed blood of Jesus enables you to **approach God** in your time of need. When you are feeling distant from God, ask the Holy Spirit to help you. Your faith must be unshakable in knowing that God does use suffering to develop in you the **character of Jesus.** Have **confidence** in your position in Christ as you draw near to your Heavenly Father.

Stronghold	Spiritual Truth
REBELLION	.*FEAR OF THE LORD*

"Therefore, since we are receiving a kingdom that cannot be shaken, let us be thankful, and so worship God acceptably with reverence and awe, for our God is a consuming fire" (Hebrews 12:28-29). *"The Lord is near to all who call on him, to all who call on him in truth. He fulfills the desires of those who fear him; he hears their cry and saves them"* (Psalm 145:18-19).

go over the strongholds material with her. Gina immediately pointed out idolatry. She could see that she had spent the entire twenty years of her marriage living a lie: pretending that they were better off than they were and maintaining an image of peace and prosperity that was far from reality. Even her walk with God had been stunted as she focused more on what others were doing in her church than on intimacy with Him and gratefulness to Him. She cried out to God, repenting of all the ways idolatry had separated her from her relationship with Him and with others. She renounced the demonic influence of the stronghold, asking God to fill her spirit with a desire to know Him more. We encouraged her to immerse herself in His Word and pray for a renewed wonder to appreciate His love and sacrifice on her behalf. She asked God to release in her a gratefulness for all He had done in her and for her. Subsequent weeks found a new peace in her home. Their financial crisis passed, and contentment replaced the greed that had so imprisoned her. Her neighbors became a source of joy to her as she deepened her relationships there and began to reflect Christ's love to them.

Pray that the Holy Spirit will restore in you an **awesome respect** of God's power and Person: God is *"the King eternal, immortal, invisible, the only God"* (see 1 Timothy 1:17). Ask that the blind area of your mind that has rebelled as Satan did to *"be like God"* (see Genesis 3:5), would instead *"see the light of the gospel of the glory of Christ, who is the image of God"* (2 Corinthians 4:4). **Stand firm** in recognizing the tempter's wiles to lure you away from the awe and reverence due our holy God, and search the Scriptures daily to reinforce a constant grateful awareness of **Who He is** and who you are.

Stronghold	Spiritual Truth

FEAR AND INSECURITY . . COURAGE, FAITH, AND TRUST

> *"The Lord is with me; I will not be afraid. What can man do to me? The Lord is with me; he is my helper. I will look in triumph on my enemies. It is better to take refuge in the Lord than to trust in man"* (Psalm 118:6-9). *"Do not fear, for I am with you; do not be dismayed, for I am your God. I will strengthen you and help you, I will uphold you with my righteous right hand"* (Isaiah 41:10). *"Peace I leave with you; my peace I give you. I do not give to you as the world gives. Do not let your hearts be troubled and do not be afraid"* (John 14:27).

Agitation from the devil blocks your absolute trust and faith in the Lordship of Christ in your life and makes you feel as if all responsibilities and decisions rest on you alone. Prayerfully relinquish all goals, activities, and outcomes into God's hands, recognizing that His goals for you are **joyful obedience** to Him and the **development of Christlikeness** as you interact with others. Begin to recognize the people He has placed in your life as **instruments of refinement** for your character. Pray that God will develop spiritual fruit in you as you choose to value individuals more highly than tasks. As you pray for the Holy Spirit to breathe into you an overwhelming sense of "holy boldness" for the sake of Jesus, you will take your eyes off your perceived inadequacies and focus on being a **faithful servant** of God. You can cast all of your worries and anxieties on God, firmly believing that He cares for you (see 1 Peter 5:7). And if you suffer for doing what is right, you can be assured that the "Spirit of glory" will rest on you!

Stronghold	Spiritual Truth

CONTROL . . . . SUBMISSION AND YIELDEDNESS

> *"Submit to one another out of reverence for Christ"* (Ephesians 5:21). *"'God opposes the proud but gives grace to the humble.' Submit yourselves, then, to God"* (James 4:6,7). *"He guides the humble in what is right and teaches them his way"* (Psalm 25:9).

God is seeking to work in you the fruit of a **gentle and reverent spirit**, which cannot coexist with a striving and manipulative one. As you yield control of your circumstances and relationships to Him, by His grace He will replace worry with trust, insensitivity with care for others, desire for recognition with a humble and contrite heart. Pray for opportunities to become an encouraging **"fan"** of others, helping them to succeed.

Stronghold	Spiritual Truth

SEXUAL IMPURITY . . . *HOLINESS*

"Since everything will be destroyed in this way, what kind of people ought you to be? You ought to live holy and godly lives as you look forward to the day of God and speed its coming...Make every effort to be found spotless, blameless and at peace with him" (2 Peter 3:11-14.) *"As obedient children, do not conform to the evil desires you had when you lived in ignorance. But just as he who called you is holy, so be holy in all you do; for it is written: 'Be holy, because I am holy'"* (1 Peter 1:14-16).

God is holy and He requires **holiness** in His people. Sexual impurity blocks the virtue of God to guide our lives: *"Without holiness no one will see the Lord"* (Hebrews 12:14). Satan knows this truth. He also knows the final judgment outcome of people who continue to live in sexual immorality. Eliminate from your life **all agents of temptation:** magazines, pictures, movies, tapes, TV — anything that can help plant a foothold in your mind. Only the Holy Spirit can help you to resist and overcome these temptations, and, through grace, draw you near to the heart of Jesus. Submit to God and **resist temptation by praying;** ask for His protection and cling to the Lord of Righteousness in trusting faith.

Stronghold	Spiritual Truth

IDOLATRY . . . . *LORDSHIP OF CHRIST*

"Since, then, you have been raised with Christ, set your hearts on things above, where Christ is seated at the right hand of God. Set your minds on things above, not on earthly things. For you died, and your life is now hidden with Christ in God" (Colossians 3:1-3). *"I do not write to you because you do not know the truth, but because you do know it and because no lie comes from the truth. See that what you have heard from the beginning remains in you. If it does, you also will remain in the Son and in the Father. And this is what he promised us — even eternal life"* (1 John 2:21,24,25).

Remember: The early Church understood that when a person was **"born again"** it meant that he had put his **full trust and reliance** in the Lord Jesus.

Go back to the basics of what drew you to the Lord: His **gift of repentance** that your sin-laden heart realized was the truth; the wonder of Jesus' **atoning sacrifice** for your sins; the gratefulness in your heart for His **forgiveness**; the newness of life as you began to yield to the Holy Spirit's **indwelling guidance** to the Father's will. These were what you heard from the beginning and knew to be the truth. **Repent** of the blindness that allowed you to love the world system — *"the cravings of sinful man, the lust of his eyes and the boasting of what he has and does"* (1 John 2:16). Put on the **Spirit of Truth** (see 1 John 4:6) to enable you to focus on the complete Lordship of Christ in your life. Pray for **discernment** to recognize the first whisper of the enemy toward self-determined decisions, distractions from God's will, inability to hear God; immediately claim the promises given to you in the Word by the Spirit.

THOUGHTS TO CONSIDER / ACTIONS TO TAKE

Conclusion

We would like to leave you with a poem given to us by our dear friend and spiritual father, Frank Murray, at a very difficult time in our walk with Jesus. We pray that its thought and meaning bless you as it has blessed us.

STEP BY STEP
"As thou goest, step by step I will open the way before thee"
(Proverbs 4:12, New Translation).

Child of My love, fear not the unknown morrow,
Dread not the new demand life makes of thee;
Thy ignorance doth hold no cause for sorrow,
Since what thou knowest not is known to Me.

Thou canst not see today the hidden meaning
Of My Command, but thou the light shalt gain;
Walk on in faith, upon My promise leaning,
And as thou goest, all shall be made plain.

One step thou seest — then go forward boldly,
One step is far enough for faith to see;
Take that, and thy next duty shall be told thee,
For step by step thy Lord is leading thee.

Stand not in fear, thine adversaries counting,
Dare every peril, save to disobey;
Thou shalt march on, all obstacles surmounting,
For I, the Strong, will open up the way.

Wherefore go gladly to the task assigned thee,
Having My promise, needing nothing more
Than just to know, where'er the future find thee,
In all thy journeying I go before.

Frank J. Exley

May God deliver you from all your strongholds and fill you with the truth of His Spirit!

Restoration Ministries

❏ **YES.** I would like to support the ministry of *Restoration Ministries* with a gift of:
$ _____.

❏ Send me information about **Demolishing Strongholds** one-day church seminars.

❏ Please put me on your mailing list.

❏ Please send me the Restoration Ministry newsletter *"Mishpachah Yeshua"* — The Family of Jesus. Yearly Subscription - Twelve issues - *Suggested Donation: $12.00*.

Your Name _____

Address _____

City _____

State _____ Postal Zip Code _____

Telephone Number (_____) _____

3595 Webb Bridge Rd. • Alpharetta, GA 30202
Telephone (770) 740-1658 • FAX (770) 442-1844

Books for Our Times

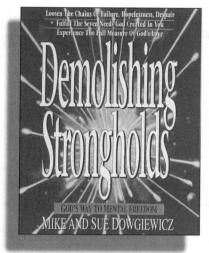

Demolishing Strongholds
Mike and Sue Dowgiewicz
Reveals how spiritual strongholds can develop and how they can be removed through Christ's power. This is a personalized workbook designed to help people recognize and combat the destructive forces of spiritual strongholds in their lives.
$15.00 softcover workbook, spiral bound
Product #336

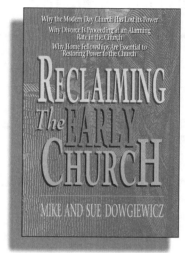

Reclaiming The Early Church
Mike and Sue Dowgiewicz
God is pouring forth a worldwide restoration of the Hebraic foundations of the early church. This book helps Christians understand what that restoration is and why it is necessary in order for Jesus to return to a church that is prepared to meet Him.
$13.95 softcover, 6x9
Product #732
August Release

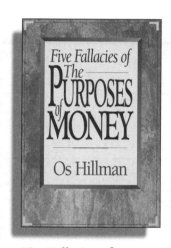

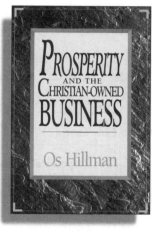

Five Fallacies of The Purposes of Money
Os Hillman
One day a series of crises entered the world of this successful advertising agency executive that would change his life forever. These life-changing events led him to discover wrong priorities and how many business people have wrongfully viewed money. Questions for reflection at the end of each section make this booklet excellent for individual or group study.
$4.95 booklet   Product #348
August Release

Adversity & Pain:
The Gifts That Nobody Wants
Os Hillman
When a crisis enters our lives how do we respond? Os Hillman was a successful executive whose world quickly changed when his marriage, business and personal finances all crashed at the same time causing him to question the reality of God. What he learned in the process will help many make sense of unexpected events that God brings into our lives.
$4.95 booklet   Product #238
August Release

Prosperity and The Christian-Owned Business
Os Hillman
Is a Christian-owned business any different than a non-Christian one? What are the characteristics of a company in which Jesus Christ is Head? Many Christian business people aspire to lead their companies in a biblical manner. Hillman describes his own journey in coming to the reality of a business that is led and directed by God.
$4.95 booklet   Product #776
August Release

Jezebel and Saul
Two of America's Most Destructive Spiritual Influences
Roger Garret,
Mike and Sue Dowgiewicz
American Christianity has been influenced by two of the most recognizable spiritual forces which have resulted in broken marriages, power struggles, and gender separation. Excellent for gender-specific groups, this study helps the reader identify these influences in his or her own life.
$4.95 booklet   Product #530
August Release.

3595 Webb Bridge Rd., Alpharetta, GA 30202
770/442-1500 FAX 770/442-1844
e-mail: Hillman.aslangroup@mindspring.com

Available at your local Christian bookstore, or call
1-800-311-2103

Resources Order Form
1-800-311-2103
Fax Orders to: (770) 442-1844

For Office Use Only
Source Code /Ext No. _____

Date of Order: _____

ASLAN GROUP PUBLISHING

3595 Webb Bridge Rd.
Alpharetta, Georgia 30202
Phone (770) 442-1003

SOLD TO

Name

Company

Address   Apt #

City, State, Zip Code

Telephone (   )
FAX (   )

SHIP TO

Name

Company

Address   Apt #

City, State, Zip Code

Telephone (   )
FAX (   )

ORDER

Quantity	Order Number	Title	Unit Price	Total Price
	336	**Demolishing Strongholds**	$15	
	732	**Reclaiming The Early Church**	$13.95	
	348	**Five Fallacies of The Purposes of Money**	$4.95	
	238	**Adversity & Pain -** *The Gifts Nobody Wants*	$4.95	
	776	**Prosperity and The Christian-Owned Business**	$4.95	
	530	**Jezebel and Saul -** *Two of America's Most Destructive Spiritual Influences*	$4.95	
	647	Restoration Ministries - **Mishpachah Newsletter** - 12 issues	$12.00	

Method of Payment:
☐ Check / Money Order / Gift Certificate / Cash   ☐ VISA   ☐ MasterCard

Payment must accompany order. Sorry, our discounts prices don't permit billing or COD. Minimum $15 order for credit cards. Overseas customers, your payment must be in U.S. bank. Canadian customers, please add 40% exchange if you pay in Canadian dollars. If you pay with a credit card, your bank will charge you the current exchange rate.

Credit Card Number – 13 or 16 digits

☐☐☐☐ ☐☐☐☐ ☐☐☐☐ ☐☐☐☐

Expiration Date: _____ / _____

Signature of Authorized Buyer: _____

Shipping

	Standard Service
Up to $20.00	$3.00
$20.01 – $55.00	$4.00
$50.01 and up	8%

Standard Service generally delivers via Post Office and require up to 3 weeks for delivery.

Sub-Total

GA Residents
Add 6% Sales Tax

Shipping

TOTAL

Notes:

Notes:

Notes:

Notes: